STO

11-8-74

"Why Me?"

"Why Me?"

Rabbi Hyman Agress

Creation House
Carol Stream, Illinois

Printed in the United States of America.

Permission granted to reprint passages from The Holy Scriptures,
Vol. I and II, © *1955 by the Jewish Publication Society.*

International Standard Book Number 0-88419-078-1
Library of Congress Catalog Card Number 73-86956

1826662

To my wife Frances,
who made this book possible

Contents

Foreword   9
Acknowledgements   21

Odyssey—Part One
The Unexpected   25
"Why Me?"   30
A Glimmer of Hope   35
Chicago   43
The Grove School   51
A New Day   55

Reflections—Part One
Shame   69
Loneliness   78
Building Bridges   85
Love and Courage   90
A Unique Child   98
The Real Michael   108
The Lighter Side   117
Discipline   122

Odyssey—Part Two
After the Grove School   131
Two Unusual Teachers   139
The Summit School   152
Closing the Circle   160

Reflections—Part Two
Looking Back   171
God's Presence   181

Milestones
The Bar Mitzvah   191
"Heal Me, O Lord"   198

Foreword

Where handicapped children are concerned, modern America behaves very much like ancient Greece. Child care among the pagan Greeks consisted of exposing sickly, deformed, and weak infants to the elements. They also exposed old folks who had lost their utility to the society, and presumably other classes of undesirables as well. Oedipus himself was left in infancy to die on the mountainside, probably because of his clubfoot (*Oedipus* means "swollen foot"), thus suggesting that the original oedipal crime was in reality attempted infanticide.

Roman philosophers continued this attitude by laughing at the Jewish tradition of caring for the weak. Martin Luther maintained the custom by recommending that retarded children be consigned to the river Moldau. More recently the Nazis included in their exterminative efforts the retarded, crippled, Gypsies, and Jews.

Many people today, perhaps a majority, feel that inmates of state mental hospitals should be sterilized, that Mongoloid children should be given minimal, if any, treatment for disease, that mercy killing of the aged is desirable, and that any measure is justified to prevent the conception and the birth of genetically defective infants. In this way, modern America

9

tends to follow in the tradition of previous empires, be they Greek, Roman, Holy Roman, German, or other.

However, the United States does differ in one significant respect, namely, the degree of candor with which it pursues these goals. Previous empires openly and directly stated their aims of elimination of segments of the population. We moderns are shocked at these cruel, if honest, views and attribute them to the uncivilized nature of man at that time. Yet even today there are contemporary South American rulers who openly declare that the maintenance of hunger and malnutrition is a political weapon, designed to deter potential revolutionary efforts.

Such attitudes—or at least the expression of such attitudes—are abhorrent to us and are considered foreign to our society. Nevertheless, in this country as well, the reality of murdering the weak continues and, in the opinion of many, has dramatically escalated in recent years. These murders are carried on consciously in some instances, unconsciously in others. Sometimes the action is rapid, at other times the death is a slow one. In some cases the sins are those of commission, in others those of omission. In both cases, however, the penalty will be the same, since history judges those who fail to prevent murder on the same side of the scale with those who actually perform the deed.

Since this reality is so uncomfortable for us to confront directly, we carry out the mission behind a screen, and it is this secrecy, this disguise of action, that distinguishes America from previous empires. The screen consists of an elaborate system of documents, pronouncements, statements of concern, conferences, institutions, programs, research, and investigation.

Thus all public documents, beginning with our earliest American history, refer to the equality and the right to life of all people. All contemporary politicians articulate their concern for the widow, the orphan, the child, the crippled, the retarded, the disturbed, the blacks, Spanish, Appalachians, Indians, and the aged. Conferences, workshops, and institutes are frequently held to discuss their plight. Pilot programs and demonstration projects are mounted, presumably to show how things should be done. Special institutions are built to contain the orphans, the retarded, the disturbed, and the aged. Blacks are likewise segregated in ghettos, Spanish-speaking in barrios, American Indians on reservations. Research studies are piled high atop each other, the whole mess growing year by year, until the classic definition of a Navajo family has become "a father, a mother, three children, and a cultural anthropologist." Government programs at all levels are initiated, revised, reorganized, scrapped, and reinstated under a new name.

A large body of "helping professionals" are recruited and trained to man this elaborate machinery. They give the image of providing, behind which lies the reality of depriving. Thus, physicians give the image of improving health, while all indices of health continue to deteriorate. Social workers provide a facade of services and financial resources, while the reality is denial of life essentials and the maintenance of poverty. Teachers appear to be giving education, but the school system continues to increase its output of illiterates and uneducated. Where the oppressed are concerned, all our social institutions work in reverse; the doctors and hospitals make them sick, the welfare system keeps them poor, and the schools make them stupid.

But this evil must be hidden, and the image of doing good must be preserved; for this purpose, another function of helping professionals can be described. Psychologists, psychiatrists, educators, pediatricians, and others combine with the mass media to play a vital role in supporting this facade of generosity. They conduct a game called Blame the Victim. Without this ploy, the populations scheduled for destruction could not be oppressed without a naked show of force. With it, the uniformed police are not necessary; rather, the victim participates in his own policing and eventually cooperates in his own downfall and death. The rules are simple, and the principle is applicable to all groups.

The first ingredient in the recipe is to weaken family supports by social, industrial, and governmental policies. It is well-recognized that our major American institutions tend to discourage and even destroy family life. Hospitals have strict visiting hours, provide few facilities for rooming-in, prevent husbands from staying with their wives during labor, and prohibit children from visiting their sick parents. Welfare agencies traditionally cut off benefits to mothers and children if a father is discovered in the house. Big business moves its executives every few years, thus uprooting family ties. American industry encourages mothers to work, but fails to provide close, convenient day care centers. The housing industry places young people in the suburbs, separated from grandparents in the inner city. Public schools try to restrict parent involvement to "safe" PTA activities—bake sales and fund raising for curtains in the teachers' lounge.

Under these societal conditions, family members inevitably begin to turn against each other. Their relationships begin to deteriorate and they begin to hate each other. Some become what society calls "emotionally disturbed." When this occurs, the helping professional accuses the mother, telling her she is hostile, rejecting, overprotective, manipulating, and domineering; he tells the father he is neglectful, distracted, self-centered, and irresponsible; he tells the brother he is rivalrous and jealous, and the son that he has not resolved his oedipal conflicts. He emphasizes the defects and deficiencies of the affected child and plays down his assets and capabilities. He blames each family member so that all will feel inadequate, inferior, passive, impotent, and responsible for their own misfortunes.

Another ingredient of the recipe is to make people poor by discriminatory taxation policies, withdrawal of housing and sanitary facilities, denial of employment, and deprivation of food. Then, blame them! Insist that they are poor because of

12

laziness and ignorance; call in the troops of professionals, therefore, to educate and motivate them. The poor can thus be brainwashed into believing they are responsible for their own plight.

If a child has retarded development or a learning disorder, again, blame the parents. Invoke fundamentalist theology, if necessary, and remind them of their sins (real or imagined) or of the sins of their parents and grandparents. Have the pediatrician ask the mother what she might have done during her pregnancy to cause this; use these questions to implant suggestive material into her thinking. Blame her for not recognizing the condition early enough, for waiting too long to consult the doctor, for shopping around for advice, for being inconsistent in management, for trying to teach her child at home, or for not teaching her child at home.

If a child's teeth decay, blame his toothbrushing habits.

The Blame the Victim game has one rule of overriding importance: Never, never blame the public, the society, the rich, the institutions, the professionals.

Never teach the poor that other people are keeping them poor.

Never teach the child with decayed teeth that the cause lies in malnutrition and poor eating habits drummed into his brain during early development by TV and advertising.

Never tell family members that family disruption has been the technique of all elite, autocratic rulers from Plato's Greece to Hitler's Germany, intended to transfer the loyalties of the father away from his son and towards his industry and corporation, the affections of the husband away from his wife and towards the army and the state.

Never inform the parent of the retarded child that the overwhelming majority of cases stem from malnutrition, economic deprivation, and brutal public schools.

Never tell the parent of the child with a learning disorder of the growing evidence that maternal anesthesia and analgesia, as well as other questionable modern obstetric practices, are important predisposing factors.

Thus the helping professional, highly trained, conscientious, dedicated, intelligent, well-motivated, carries out the necessary steps in the Blame the Victim game. This enables the killing to continue under cover of the image of providing services. It is this characteristic—the separation of image from reality by a highly developed social structure—that distinguishes American oppression from others, past and present.

Against this grim backdrop appears Rabbi Hyman Agress and his family. He brings with him the baggage of generations of Old Testament devotees. That baggage consists of adherence to biblical ethics and values. In contrast to ancient pagan morality, the Bible makes no distinction between persons. All people are equal; all are entitled to life; the physically handicapped, mentally retarded, and emotionally disturbed have the same nobility as the handsome and beautiful people. Jewish values do not include population restriction but rather its very opposite: "Be fruitful and multiply."

The Jewish view of welfare is best exemplified by the scene from the musical *Fiddler on the Roof* where the beggar approaches the rich man for his weekly handout. When told that business wasn't so good, he responds indignantly, "Just because you had a bad week, I should suffer?" Jewish beggars have a claim on the rich! Old Testament ethics stress the responsibilities of the wealthy and the fortunate. The child with a learning disorder has a legitimate claim on society!

Rabbi Agress' story begins with his three-year-old son Michael. There is a typical series of nightmarish experiences with modern medicine, including the usual encounters with impersonal physicians, indifferent specialists, conflicting laboratory tests, delayed diagnoses, confused counseling, and inadequate follow-up.

Michael was placed on drugs in an attempt to alter his behavior. Medications such as amphetamines (Dexedrine) and methylphenidate (Ritalin) are today being given to hundreds of thousands of children supposedly brain-damaged. Yet the rabbi's story demonstrates the futility of the drug approach and the crucial necessity of the human approach. In spite of this obvious truth, the logic of American society as described earlier dictates that more and more such children will be produced, fewer human resources will be devoted to their care and rehabilitation, and therefore more and more will have to be drugged. Parents such as the Agresses will be conned into blaming themselves, their marriage, their parents, and their in-laws. Their subsequent guilt will make many like them willing partners in a growing conspiracy of doctors, teachers, and parents to drug our nation's children.

Rabbi Agress finally finds help almost by accident through a chance conversation with one of his congregants who happens to be a pediatrician. This is one of the few satisfactory facilities he encounters. In keeping with the need to project a good image, our country usually seems to meet about five percent of the need. Such model institutions receive adequate funding and wide publicity.

These models carry out a number of valuable functions for the establishment. First, by virtue of the publicity, they delude the public into believing that such care is available to all. Second, they affect professionals in the same field and other institutions striving to the same end who have been less successful; they affect them by creating feelings of inferiority at being unable to similarly accomplish such a high level of success. Yet it is perfectly obvious to the outside, objective observer that the resources are not available to the other ninety-five percent, and furthermore, other circumstances are not similar.

These models take the cream of the helping professionals—the most capable, articulate, industrious, the ones best able to manipulate, the craftiest "grantsmen"—and keep them busy with their small programs, self-satisfied with their efforts. Without the model programs, these people would suffer from great frustration, and would in all likelihood be leading the troops in the kinds of maneuvers and strategy designed to secure sufficient resources to insure services for all. Thus, in a society bent on denying services surreptitiously, the model program and demonstration project play a vital role. Needless to say, these projects are never, never converted into mass-action programs. The goal in contemporary society of extending a good project to the entire needy population remains as elusive as the medieval pursuit of the Holy Grail. Of course, the seekers of the modern Holy Grail derive substantial profit, since a good demonstration project can convert an assistant professor into a full professor, and a successful pilot program can insure a department chairmanship in an elite university.

The Agresses go through the maze of the modern American medical establishment with its irrelevance, ineptness, scare techniques, and actual dangers. The psychiatrist is required to pronounce them sane; the pediatrician is a BusyDoctor; the gynecologist terrifies Mrs. Agress over a benign lump in the breast; the social worker tongue-lashes them with the accusation, "Can't you see he's retarded?" and the neurologist and psychologist join the social worker in a chorus of cold, impersonal pessimism and a demand that they "accept his condition." The special school educational staff recommend a "parentectomy"—that the parents not see or visit Michael for a year. Almost all the special schools they visit have criteria for admission that exclude more applicants than they include.

The Agresses face the diagnostic nightmare with experts fighting over brain damage, retardation, perceptual handicap, emotional disturbance, learning disorder. The medieval alchemists and practitioners of polypharmacy exhibit about the same degree of skill and probably more compassion. As a matter of fact, the diagnostic criteria remind one of the medieval debates about how many angels could dance on the head of a pin. The tragedy is that in any case management has practically no relation to the diagnostic category—as the Agresses finally discover.

They also face the educational establishment with its ar-

Foreword

rogance, expensiveness, private-public dichotomy, confusion, ignorance, and coldness. When Michael finally reaches a "good" school, he learns to read by himself. Again, the modern American school is revealed as a cunning device to prevent thinking and learning while giving the image of promoting those ends. Many, perhaps all, of our present functionally illiterate children would learn to read by themselves were it not for the antireading policies and practices of schools. Illiteracy is built into the system, and as a matter of fact, the production and maintenance of illiteracy in certain population groups may be considered as one of the primary—if not *the* primary—goal of American education. Whether this results from conscious or unconscious motivation is of little importance to the affected child or adult. Those responsible for the present system are acting either from ignorance or venality, and as time moves on and information becomes more widely dispersed, it becomes increasingly more plausible that the real architects of our schools, our medical system, and our welfare system are motivated by selfish, evil purposes. The inevitable result— namely, destruction of themselves as well as of their victims— is not sufficiently appreciated to modify their sinister activities and behavior.

Even when Michael learns to read by himself, to recite the Sabbath *Kiddush* ritual and other prayers, the establishment continues to play the Blame the Victim game. Doctors ask, "How do you know? Perhaps he has only learned to sound words." Thus both the parents and the child are depreciated in the continuing attempt to convince them of their own inadequacy and to brainwash them into accepting the domination of the experts and their ruling-class allies. Rabbi Agress utilizes his Jewish background to defend against this kind of attack with the ancient precept, "Be not wicked in your own eyes." In this aspect, as in many others, his appreciation and knowledge of Jewish tradition becomes invaluable in beating off the pagan and barbarian onslaughts of our culture.

The Agresses learn for themselves the elements to which

17

professionals attach fancy titles—*operant conditioning, graded curriculum, structured situation.* They also learn that master's degrees and certification are no guarantees of excellence, although they are not yet aware of the almost inverse relationship between modern schooling and competence. They learn that love is more effective in calming a child than medication, a truth yet to be discovered by modern science. They learn to appreciate the value of meeting with parents of other handicapped children. Parents' groups are still in their infancy stage and are mostly limited to diseases that affect rich as well as poor—poliomyelitis, cystic fibrosis, nephrosis, leukemia. Diseases that affect only the poor—lead poisoning, sickle cell anemia, malnutrition—are not represented among the list of parents' organizations. Too many obstacles are placed in the path of poor people wishing to organize themselves. Parent organizations for mentally handicapped children—retarded, disturbed, perceptually damaged—have made dramatic progress in recent years. But they have a long way to go before even modest goals can be reached. Parents must first strengthen each other by transferring the burden of guilt back to the society—and its agents, the helping professionals—who have tried to shift it to parents. They can then move ahead to discipline the schools, educate the doctors, and threaten the legislators. These activities can be clothed in elegant terminology such as *orientation, involvement, influence,* and *lobbying.* But, if the aggressor does not respond, the basic law of self-preservation in the face of attack still applies. A strong parents' organization can effectively load the gun and point it at those who continue to deprive and thus kill their children.

When parents of mentally handicapped children finally combine with other deprived people—blind, deaf, physically handicapped, racial minorities, old folks, unemployed—then the roar of their combined firearms can finally rid them of the modern Pharaohs who from the insulation of their palaces withhold the straw and mortar and then blame the children and parents for not building more palaces.

The Agresses learn how valuable their handicapped child is. This may well be the hardest lesson for parents of retarded and similarly affected children, especially in a society that regards them as less than people and is now tooling up to kill them on a large scale sometime between conception and birth. This killing, dressed up in fancy terms such as *genetic counseling* and *human engineering*, may threaten the well-being and lives of some normal fetuses; but no matter, no price is too high to pay for the prevention of the birth of a handicapped child. The techniques of animal and plant breeding are thus applied—in the name of humanity!—to people.

Rabbi Agress beautifully and accurately describes the civilizing effect such a child has on his family and therefore on the world. I can almost hear some bright, ambitious scientist argue that, if that is the case, why don't we try to increase the number of retarded children? And I can hardly wait to answer him that that is precisely what he and his colleagues are presently accomplishing and are unwittingly planning to extend in the future.

Another deep lesson finally learned by the rabbi and his wife is that history is important. America is an ahistorical, even antihistorical country. We have a tradition of rejecting our past, or at least disregarding it. This attitude must inevitably be on collision course with the Jewish view emphasizing the supreme importance of history and the absolute necessity of remembering. This kind of reeducation is essential for the survival of oppressed people in a society determined to acculturate them at all costs. Thus, Latins, in order to survive, must speak Spanish at home; Greeks, Greek; blacks, patios; and Poles, Polish. Parents of handicapped children must emphasize their children's differences from others rather than their similarities. The prescription for survival might read, "Recognize, respect, and emphasize your own identity; your interests are not the same as those of the majority. Either you separate yourself as a distinct entity with special claims, or you try to merge into the background and thus give up the struggle to secure the special needs for your own survival and growth."

For the rabbi and his family, Judaism, with its eternal optimism, provides the necessary life jackets. Unlike the ancient Greeks, Jewish tradition has always regarded each human being as equally valuable. This tradition has permeated Jewish legislation and community practices throughout the ages. The Old Testament is essentially a slave document, emphasizing as it does the rights of widows, orphans, poor, enslaved, and weak. Thus, its teachings place it at variance with Greek, Roman, Egyptian, Babylonian, and much of modern American civilizations.

Rabbi Agress' book will be valuable to all other parents with perceptually handicapped children. It should be required reading for teachers, doctors, and psychologists. But, realistically speaking, few of them will even look at it. His personal experiences and views should also provide instruction and encouragement for local residents of Chicago and suburbs, for fellow Jews, for Christians, for parents of children with other kinds of handicaps, and for "plain" people.

Many parents will find themselves helped by Rabbi Agress. Some will feel that, having passed these milestones, they are in a position to further help him. Most parents probably are at about the same stage as the Agresses, and they will be especially grateful for this narrative.

ROBERT S. MENDELSOHN, M.D., F.A.A.P.
Associate Professor, Department of Preventive Medicine
and Community Health
University of Illinois, College of Medicine

Pediatric Consultant, Department of Mental Health
State of Illinois

Coeditor, American Medical Association
Handbook on Mental Retardation

Acknowledgements

I gratefully acknowledge the help of the following people:

Virginia Matson, who created and guided the Grove School, helped to educate Michael, encouraged me in writing this book, and contacted the publishers. Without her this book would not exist.

Dr. Robert Mendelsohn, who read the manuscript and graciously agreed to write a foreword.

Jesse Jacobs, a dear friend who initially edited the manuscript, unmercifully eliminating what he referred to as "sermonic hot air."

Dr. Morris Fishbein, who thought highly of the work and sent it to his publishers.

Dr. Robert Webber and Jane Nelson, my editors, who battled for the publication of this work.

Dale Mindell, a friend, congregant, and fine poet who read the work and offered some valuable suggestions.

Rabbi Judah Nadich, who was kind enough to comment on the book and suggest certain changes.

Monzell Himes and Anita Kemper, my secretaries, who worked many an hour deciphering my almost illegible handwriting and typing the manuscript.

And Dean Merrill, who applied the final, vital editing touches.

To all these people I say thank you, and God bless you.

Odyssey—Part One

1
The Unexpected

My own smug little world crumbled on Tuesday, October 16, 1962. Frances and I were taking our Michael to the pediatrician for his yearly checkup. Michael was three years old then, a beautiful child. His eyes sparkled, he laughed easily and was always smiling even at strangers. People would stop us in the street to say, "What a beautiful, friendly child he is." Lately we had been a bit nervous about his development. He did not walk until he was twenty months. At three he could only say a few words, although he had always been able to make his wants crystal clear. But he seemed so alert, and we had always found comfort in Dr. Spock's admonishments that each child develops differently, and parents need not be concerned with the slow maturer.

After the examination, the pediatrician asked us to step into his private office and suggested that we sit down. "There is something seriously wrong with this boy," he said in a precise, clinical fashion. "He might well have some brain damage." He could not assure us that Michael would ever learn to speak or read or write. He strongly urged us to have him evaluated by a neurologist. He could suggest a very competent one.

A week later, John F. Kennedy told the American people that Russia had installed missiles in Cuba and that the United

25

States would therefore blockade Cuba until these missiles were withdrawn. It seemed that the world was threatened with extinction; everyone was anxiously watching television, listening to the radio, or reading newspapers.

How ironic! My world had ended a week earlier, when I had heard *brain-damaged* and *retarded*. What horribly cruel words these were! Frances and I were young; I was thirty and she twenty-three. We thought we were very mature, but we had never really come face to face with such an overwhelming problem. Both my parents were living, as were hers. In fact, even her grandparents, in their eighties and married over sixty years, were still very alert. Both of us had had illnesses in our families, but there had been no tragic aftereffects. We were young. We had done nothing wrong, I reasoned. God had been with us, and He would continue to look after us.

Now that I look back to 1962 (it seems a lifetime), I realize what a naive view of God and religion this was. How dare I assume that the world existed solely for my benefit—to cater to my every want?

It is almost impossible to describe the spiritual, psychological, and even physical torment that Frances and I went through for seven days and nights until the scheduled consultation with the neurologist. We were torn between conflicting emotions and expectations. We dreaded the blackest of prognoses. We feared that Michael would grow up with the mentality of a two-year-old—little more than a vegetable, unable to feed or toilet-train himself, or to speak. Other times we would spin the fanciest of daydreams—the pediatrician would be proven wrong; the neurologist would say that Michael was completely normal. Perhaps the doctor could prescribe some magical medicine, and Michael would begin to speak. Or perhaps he would find a small growth pressing against Michael's brain, and wondrous brain surgery could cure him. Finally, we would discover that all this was a hideous nightmare from which we would shortly awake.

We told no one of our visit to the pediatrician, neither our parents nor our dearest friends. We were completely alone and isolated in our misery and fear. I could not summon the courage to go with my wife and Michael to the neurologist. I stayed home to baby-sit with our younger son Steve, pacing the floor, praying and torturing myself by alternately hoping for the best and expecting the worst. When Frances finally returned, I knew the results without even asking.

The neurologist could not say how much further Michael would mature mentally, what his development would be like, or even if he would ever learn to talk. He had used the term "Possibly borderline retarded." How retarded? Only time would tell. Another loud thud, another crash of our world, but this time not unexpectedly.

The neurologist wanted Michael to undergo a battery of tests, x-rays of the brain, an electroencephalogram, and various blood tests. However, he did not anticipate any findings that would alter his diagnosis. Our pediatrician would inform us of the results and prescribe medication.

For three weeks, Frances took Michael almost daily to the outpatient division of a large hospital. She soon learned how cold, frightening, and impersonal these institutions can be. Michael was terribly afraid of the tests, the surroundings, the pain and discomfort. He cried and yelled in the hospital corridors, the waiting rooms, and during the actual examinations and tests. Yet no nurses or doctors tried to calm or soothe him or utter a word of comfort to the distraught mother. In fact, at times Frances felt as if she were being criticized for not controlling Michael. It was a three-week nightmare.

Finally we had our appointment with the pediatrician. He briefly detailed the results of the tests. They had shown nothing new. All were negative. He reaffirmed his and the neurologist's diagnoses and prescribed medication. One of Michael's major problems was hyperactivity. We were to learn that hyperactivity is one of the telltale signs of brain damage or brain dysfunction, and that the hyperactive child has a very short span of attention. He cannot sit still; he must constantly move. His thought processes and his actions are disorganized; he can be quite destructive, breaking toys and household furnishings. Michael had all the manifestations of the hyperactive child. Our pediatrician gave us a drug which he said might help his hyperactivity.

I vividly recall the results of one drug. The prescribed dosage had had little, if any, effect. Our pediatrician suggested that we increase the dosage. It was a Friday evening, and we gave Michael a whole pill instead of the half he had been receiving. He began to sob, run around, and bang his head against the wall. It was one of the most terrifying scenes I have ever experienced. It seemed as if he was going stark, raving mad! There was no controlling him. We tried desperately to call our doctor, but the line was either busy or there was no answer.

Finally Michael quieted down and fell asleep. Now I wonder if he had not experienced what we have come to call a "bad trip." At that time, however, we knew next to nothing about the possible side effects of various drugs, and no doctor had mentioned them to us.

The weeks wore on. My father retired as the rabbi of a small synagogue in Brooklyn. It had been his lifelong dream eventually to resettle in the Holy Land. He had been married there some forty-one years before, but had been forced by the Depression and Arab riots to flee to the United States. Now they planned to return to Israel, buy an apartment, and live comfortably on their savings plus Social Security.

Michael's condition cast a shadow upon their plans. They wanted to remain near us, but we persuaded them that they should not abandon their cherished dreams. For six months my father was gloriously happy in the Holy Land. We received lengthy, beautifully written letters describing his feelings and always concluding with the hope that God would help Michael. Then I received a telegram that father was dying of cancer, and before I could fly to Israel, he was dead.

28

The Unexpected

Three years later, Frances' father also died of cancer. We have had our share of illness and death. Yet none of these troubles, deaths, and sorrows has had a traumatic effect comparable to the news of Michael's brain damage. The doctor's words and the mental torment that followed shattered the hopes and dreams I had nurtured since childhood. I was enveloped by a feeling of helplessness and hopelessness, compounded by the seeming indifference of Michael's pediatrician and neurologist. I felt terribly alone, isolated from the companionship of my friends and acquaintances. I was afflicted by alternate emotions of shame and guilt. But most devastating of all was the effect of this crisis upon my spiritual well-being. The very foundations of my faith had been shaken, and my beliefs seemed to be shattered beyond repair. I felt myself sinking into a black abyss, forsaken by man and God.

2
"Why Me?"

My spiritual upheaval began with an intense absorption in prayer, a search for a God who would cure Michael and end the nightmare.

That very first day, I left the doctor's office, got into my Ford, sat, and stared at the ignition for what seemed an eternity. Finally turning the key, I drove home, all the while thinking to myself, *Wouldn't it solve everything if I had an accident and died? Wouldn't this horrible nightmare finally be over?* During the half-hour drive home, neither Frances nor I said a word to each other nor shed one tear. Crying would come later, after the initial shock wore off. At this moment, I felt totally lost and alone, cut off from all humanity, unable to find a modicum of comfort or warmth in my wife's nearness or in our shared grief.

That afternoon I walked into the temple to pray. I walked to the holy ark, drew the curtain, opened its doors, stared at the Torah scrolls, the first five books of the Bible— and I prayed to God. I prayed that our pediatrician was completely wrong, that Michael was as smart as any normal youngster, that God would not forsake me but would miraculously heal Michael. I prayed, using my own words, and I cried. When I finished praying and crying, I could feel within me a warmth emanating from my heart and traveling through my body, bringing with it a sense of calm and hope. God would help me, I was sure of that. I was not alone.

The week that followed was a time of feverishly mixed emotions. Long hours of gloom and depression were punctuated by moments of sunny optimism. Periods of anxiety were followed by prayer and the comforting thought: *surely God will answer my prayers and this hellish nightmare will abruptly end.*

All this stopped with the neurologist's confirmation of the initial diagnosis. I had turned to God and He had not answered me.

For the next few months I continued to minister to the needs of my congregation, but in a daze. I prayed every morning, phylacteries upon my head and left arm as has been the practice of the traditional Jew for the past two thousand years. But I did it all quite automatically and almost painfully. I would recite the morning prayer: "Thou sustainest the living with loving-kindness, and in great mercy callest the departed to everlasting life. Thou upholdest the falling, healest the sick, settest free those in bondage, and keepest faith with those that sleep in the dust." I would think to myself, *Where is Thy loving-kindness, or Thy healing?*

It became obvious to me that the very foundation of my faith had been brought into question and was crumbling. Was it possible that I, a rabbi, the son of a rabbi, had lived for thirty years guided by basic spiritual premises that I really did not understand and could no longer accept?

Since my early teens I had taken for granted the fact that I would ultimately study for ordination and serve a congregation as a rabbi. I had never felt what is sometimes referred to among certain Christian denominations as a "calling." This term cannot truly apply to the functions of a rabbi. The Hebrew term *rabbi* means master or teacher; the rabbi serves his congregation best when he can effectively act as a teacher to both the young and their parents. I had always enjoyed teaching, and I looked forward to the time when I, as a rabbi, could educate a group of Jews in their ancient faith and perhaps strengthen, to some degree, their belief in God and their loyalty to Judaism.

How could I strengthen someone else's faith when my own had been shaken? How could I respond to another's anguished cry of "Why me?" when I lay in my bed at night torturing myself with the same question?

Certain phrases are used both by children and adults and yet have very different meanings. One of these phrases is "Why me?" The child says it petulantly. "Why blame me for breaking the bike? Why do I have to clean my room today? Why shouldn't Mike or Alexandra do the work?"

But when an adult uses these words, they can be the most tormented utterances imaginable. It is a cry in the dark, a howl in the night. It may not even be vocalized. Many a night I lay thinking it, yet not daring to say the words, "Why me?" I had been conditioned since childhood, both by my parents and by my religious training, to associate "Why me?" with having done something wrong. Sin brought with it retribution; punishment followed the commission of a crime. Therefore, if I suffered, there was obviously good cause for this suffering. Perhaps I had done something awful, committed an unpardonable sin, and God was punishing me in this manner.

Yet logically this just could not be so. I hope I am not so arrogant as to think I have never sinned or need not be ashamed of anything I have done. Yet am I truly so evil that I need to be punished in this fashion? Does not the Bible describe God as a just and merciful Deity? In the classic words of Abraham's appeal to God, "Shall not the Judge of all the earth do justly?" Have I not been bidden to view God as a loving Father? Most disturbing of all—what sin had Michael committed to be thus afflicted?

My years as a clergyman had been hard work. Frances had

been tempted at times to reintroduce me to our children: "Mike, Steve, meet your dad." There were moments when I had felt disheartened, when progress seemed to be agonizingly slow, my dreams for my congregation unfulfilled. And there were other times when I felt that the rabbinate could be the most rewarding and beautifully meaningful of all professions. Those were the days when I thought to myself that I had truly been doing God's work, when some word or deed of mine had affected one of my congregants, when a sermon had hit home, had forced those who were listening to do some thinking, perhaps even to begin searching their souls. The response might not have been complimentary; a congregant may have said, "You know, rabbi, I didn't agree with your sermon this morning." But at least I knew he hadn't fallen asleep, and that I had, in fact, forced him to react, to think.

There were also those agonizing moments that are part of every clergyman's existence. The times when I had to find the words to comfort a father who had lost his young son or daughter, or a young widow who had held her dying husband in her arms and now must find some reason to continue living. I felt that I must be so very careful in my attempt to console the bereaved. I must be prepared to respond to the bitter cry of a mother as she asked, "Why did this happen to me? Why me?" There had even been occasions when I had reacted inwardly to this cry with a sense of impatience and frustration. *Why ask me?* I had thought. *Am I God?* Yet, at the same time I also realized, *This woman isn't accusing me. I'm her sounding board. I am a tangible symbol of her faith. I am being asked to justify her faith and my own, and I must answer not only this woman but myself. In a very real and personal sense I am being asked to exonerate the supreme Judge of us all.*

In a much broader sense, I, a clergyman living, thinking, and preaching in the second half of the twentieth century, recognized the fact that the cry of "Why me?" had been elevated to cosmic proportions. The optimism and hope of the nineteenth century had degenerated into the mass annihilation and slaughter of the twentieth. As a Jew, I lived in the shadow of the crematories of Auschwitz, Bergen-Belsen, and Dachau, and I had to ask myself "Why me?" Why was I the fortunate Jewish boy whose parents had left Russia and Poland before the advent of Hitler? Was I more worthy, more innocent, or more clever than the three million Jewish children who perished?

As an American I lived under the specter of the mushroom cloud that had obliterated Hiroshima and Nagasaki and could easily end all civilization. As a citizen of the world, I knew of the starving children in Africa and India and the innocent victims of the tragic war in Vietnam.

The theological storm of those years that was popularly called the God-is-dead movement was in large measure a response to the horrible experiences of the Second World War, the brutality of the Nazi and communist regimes, the increase in our destructive capabilities, and the seeming impossibility of learning to live at peace with each other. In part, it was a black answer to the metaphysical question, "If there is a God in the heavens, how could He have allowed this to happen?"

All these diverse problems had now, five years after my ordination, become terribly relevant to me. Michael was diagnosed as having brain damage. Why did this happen to him? Why did this happen to me?

I felt totally bereft and alone. The very foundation of my faith and my life's work was shaken. *Where was God?* And then came the tragically insinuating doubt: *Is there a God?*

34

3
A Glimmer of Hope

Michael's pediatrician, the professional to whom Frances and I instinctively turned both for hope and help, seemed to epitomize the typical busy, big-city medical practitioner. He could be reached by telephone only between eight and eight-thirty in the morning and six-thirty to seven in the evening. He would answer at other times, but unless the call proved to be an emergency there was a two-dollar charge for disturbing the doctor during working hours.

Since he had a large practice, it was difficult, if not impossible, to reach him during the prescribed half-hours. When she had to phone about a medication, Frances would start dialing exactly as the second hand reached eight and would call every fifteen seconds until finally there was no busy signal. More often than not she spent the half-hour in total frustration, never getting through. She would then have to start the whole process over in the evening. Appointments had to be made weeks in advance unless Michael was critically ill. Needless to say, there were no house calls.

Perhaps this is the only way a doctor can function in a large city with so many children. But I couldn't help feeling that he wasn't really very interested in Michael and his future well-being or in Frances and me as the parents of a hyperactive,

35

brain-damaged child. Michael was just another one of his many dozens to be weighed, measured, examined, and inoculated. The drugs he prescribed were either largely ineffective or else so potent as to cause him to cry, yell, and bang his head. If possible, Michael was wilder and more uncontrollable than he had been before we discovered that he was handicapped. We were to learn much later that this increased hyperactivity was in large measure a response to our own altered emotional outlook and our changed attitude toward Michael. Our inner turmoil and confusion, my own sense of guilt and shame toward my child, and at times, my very hatred of him, communicated to Michael, and he became more unmanageable, drawing even more tightly into his shell.

At this most crucial of times, I had a chance conversation with one of my congregants, a young woman married to an attorney, the mother of two small children; she was a pediatrician on a leave of absence from one of New York's municipal hospitals. I had dropped by her home one weekday evening to discuss some congregational matters with her and her husband. During our conversation, for some inexplicable reason, I started to blurt out my troubles with Michael. No member of my congregation knew about his problem; I had told no one, because I was too ashamed and confused. Yet sitting in this apartment, talking to her husband (she was listening with half an ear as she busied herself putting her two children to bed), I found myself compulsively telling them my troubles and heartache. I told them of my shock at the initial news of Michael's handicap, of my confusion and helplessness, and above all, of the pediatrician's seeming indifference to Michael.

Did I hope that this couple would help me? Not in the usual sense of the word. I truly believed that Michael was hopeless and I had no intention of going from doctor to doctor or from clinic to clinic searching for a different diagnosis. However, I had kept these problems tightly confined in my heart and mind for so very long that I was in danger of destroying myself. I had to tell someone about Michael, and it seemed easier to speak of him to a professional pediatrician who would comprehend the situation without any need to elaborate.

The doctor and her husband listened for about ten minutes and then she interrupted the flow of my words by saying, "I don't know if I can help you. You have a pediatrician who is probably quite competent. But I can give you the name of a medical center where you could take Michael. I did some work there, and they have a very fine evaluation program for handicapped children. I'll help you get an appointment. Go there! They may be able to help you."

I had mixed emotions as Frances took Michael for his first appointment at the Albert Einstein Medical Center. I couldn't bear the thought of yet another doctor saying, "Michael's retarded, and I cannot tell you how far he will go intellectually or whether he will ever learn to talk." And yet . . . perhaps, perhaps this time the answer would be different. Most important of all, I owed Michael this opportunity.

Frances returned smiling for the first time in three months. She had not met with the doctor or been given any good news, but her treatment at the center had been so gentle and considerate that she felt warmed by their kindness. Her first appointment had been with a psychiatric social worker who took down a detailed history of Michael's birth and behavior. Michael had been in the room with them, aimlessly wandering from object to object. Instead of treating him as a nuisance or a freak, this woman had spent time talking and even playing with him, smiling at him, and saying to Frances, "What a beautiful child he is."

The following week Frances and Michael met with a child psychiatrist. Once again, the meeting was gratifying. The psychiatrist was patient with Michael, allowing him to wander about and touch whatever he wanted, do whatever came into his mind. He calmly answered any question Frances asked, and reassured her.

The last appointment was with a pediatric neurologist who

was the head of the evaluation team. He examined Michael and then set a date for a private consultation with us. At this final meeting, he would sum up the findings of the team.

We met the neurologist in the first week of May. It had been a terribly long and torturous six months. We had prepared ourselves for the worst; yet we entered the doctor's office with a certain sense of hope engendered by the atmosphere created in the hospital and the kind consideration shown Frances. These people were not cold professionals. They were human beings who cared.

As I sat down facing the neurologist, I thought to myself, *I'm not really scared. This man can't tell me anything more or worse than I have already assumed.* As it turned out, the results of the evaluation were not as bad as I had imagined.

"We're not at all sure of Michael," he began. "He may be retarded because of damage to his brain. But it is also possible that he is suffering from an emotional disorder. He may not want to speak for some deep psychological reason.

"However, an emotional disorder will not make the problem any easier. He may never talk, even if his intelligence is normal or above normal. We can't give you any definite answers.

"I would, nevertheless, suggest some things that you may want to do. First, get rid of his pills. I've never met a hyperactive youngster who was helped by drugs. Secondly, if you want to, we will try to place him in a nursery school under the direction of our medical center. The nursery meets twice a week for two hours a day. We can observe Michael more closely in the nursery, and the teacher may be able to help both you and him. It's too late to start this semester. But you can start him in the fall."

I left the office that morning with a feeling in my heart that had been absent for months—hope. He had not reassured us about Michael, but he *had* emphasized and reemphasized the fact that Michael puzzled the team. His words had given us hope. They would continue to observe him. A group of professionals were interested in Michael's well-being. They even had a nursery for him. Frances and I would receive help. We were not alone!

The summer months passed quickly. Michael seemed to be a wee bit quieter and less hyperactive without the drugs or tranquilizers. In the first week of September we brought him to the nursery school. The director and supervisor was a most unusual woman who was to have a profound influence on our lives. The nursery school was divided into two groups. The first was composed of children suffering from cerebral palsy; Michael's group had four children, hyperactive, unable to speak or else barely able to say a few words, and quite incapable of playing with each other in any meaningful way. The sessions were only two hours long. One or two of the mothers usually remained in the supervisor's office for the period. The supervisor spent part of her time with the children and part with the parents discussing various problems. She was a psychiatric social worker who had been "in analysis," as she told us on more than one occasion, for two years, and she fancied herself as somewhat of a psychoanalyst. She was also a woman of definite and strong opinions, willing and able to share them with others; she was constantly analyzing the parents, their sex life, marital relationships, frigidity, and the oedipal complexes of their children. She assumed that the children's problems were caused by the parents' hang-ups. Many a day Frances returned home in a hysterical state, convinced that our marriage was on the rocks, that her relationship with her parents was bad, and that my mother (who had just become a widow and was planning to visit us from Israel) was an ogre.

She also attempted to convince all the parents to visit a psychiatrist. Inasmuch as Frances and I thought of ourselves as modern adults, we naturally followed her suggestion and made an appointment at the local mental health clinic. Our first meeting with the psychiatrist was a joint one followed by individual appointments. Afterward, he met with both of us once again to sum up his findings: we both seemed to function relatively well without psychiatric aid; our problem with Michael was quite obviously going to be a great source of anxiety; he had no objections to seeing us on a private basis, provided we paid the usual fee, but he didn't feel that this was really necessary.

Frances and I were now certified sane by a psychiatrist.

Yet the supervisor was very effective with Michael. She treated him as a normal child with some problems. She was firm with him. She expected that he act his age. She took no nonsense from him. For the first time we saw results. She also worked with Frances and me, trying to convince us that it was vital for us as parents to show some backbone—a firm attitude towards our children. With time we learned to distinguish between her positive suggestions and negative advice. She disturbed us with her opinions, strongly presented and based upon an amateurish knowledge of Freud. But she gave us two ingredients that we desperately needed at the time and for which we have been thankful ever since: hope and help for Michael. In later years, after we had left New York, we fully realized the true implications of her aid.

Michael attended the nursery school for one year. During that time an idea began to germinate in our minds. We wanted to move to Chicago, though not into the city proper. My father was dead, my mother was in Israel, and I had lost contact with old friends. Frances' parents and her brother lived in Chicago. At this critical time in our lives we wanted to be near our family in a real, physical sense.

In addition, Frances had always disliked the city. She hated the crowds, the shoving in the subway stations, trains, and department stores, the brusqueness and at times downright rudeness of the people, the large apartment houses rising like monsters from concrete floors, the constant losing battle against dirt and pollution. To her the city was cold and its inhabitants even more frigid.

As a native-born New Yorker, I had grown hardened to the city's noise, dirt, crowds, and indifference, and I hoped that my parents, friends, and the educational and cultural advantages—the theater, opera, museums—would compensate for its disadvantages. They didn't. I had little money to spend on theater or opera. I now disliked the city as intensely as Frances did.

Finally, a bit of superstition crept into our decision. We thought of this city as the place of our troubles. Michael had been diagnosed here. At Frances' yearly checkup, the gynecologist had found a lump in her breast. Thank God, it was benign, but the week before surgery was a nightmare. There is a Jewish proverb, "If one changes one's place, one changes one's luck."

I began to look for a rabbinical position near Chicago. I followed the usual procedure and was fortunate in finding that the temple in Aurora, Illinois, a far western suburb of Chicago, had an opening. On a summer morning in July, 1964, a year and a half after we first learned of Michael's brain damage, we moved.

One problem remained: What were we to do with Michael? We had finally found some help; could we find such help in Chicago? The staff at the medical school assured us that we could. They had a very fine evaluation clinic in mind and were sure that Michael's placement would be no problem.

After moving, we often thought back to the nursery school at the medical center. Frances had become friends with two of the other mothers. We had all become attached to the children, so lovable, yet so handicapped and helpless. We also wondered about the supervisor. Was she still there? Was she still as friendly, yet opinionated?

We eventually went back for a month's vacation. New York was still as large, dirty, and boisterous as before, but we didn't mind it as much. We no longer lived there. We were now tourists.

One Friday we drove out to visit the nursery. We found our supervisor, as friendly and strong as ever. Then we asked her about the children. One had gone off to public school. The second was attending a school for the mentally retarded. And the third one, who had seemed so much like Michael, hyperactive, destructive at times, a beautiful, lovable boy, far more physically coordinated than Michael, where was he? He had been institutionalized.

4
Chicago

A rabbi's first year in a new position is usually the most trying, while at the same time the most exciting. There are so many new members to meet, families to visit, friends to make. He must begin planning the year's educational programs: the adult classes to be taught, and in many positions, such as mine, where he is also principal of the religious school, he must project a curriculum for the following year, interview and hire teachers, and purchase books.

Also, a rabbi usually assumes a new position in late summer. This may make it easier for the family to move, but it plunges him almost immediately into the busiest part of his year—the High Holy Days in September or, at the latest, the beginning of October. It is during the High Holy Days that the rabbi meets and preaches to the largest number of congregants. He must therefore, particularly with a new congregation, spend a good deal of time preparing the services and at least four sermons, perhaps the only sermons a majority of his congregation will hear during the whole year.

In Aurora, I faced an even busier year. I had decided to take courses toward a Ph.D. and had been accepted as a graduate student at the University of Chicago.

Yet I looked forward to the new year with a good deal of excitement, even some joy. Frances' parents were an hour's drive away. The western part of Aurora, in which the temple is located, has attractive homes, wide lawns, trees, flowers, and bushes—everything we hadn't had in New York. Frances enthusiastically set to work making the parish house our home.

Everything seemed ideal but for one major problem— Michael. How were we to care for him? Where would he receive an education? In the fall he would be five years old. A normal five-year-old would be starting kindergarten. We could not comprehend the possibility of Michael attending a normal kindergarten. He didn't speak, nor was he capable of sitting still or playing with children.

But we were not without hope. The Einstein Medical Center had given us the name of a highly recommended evaluation center. We were certain they would help us. Frances soon called for an appointment.

I was completely unprepared for the shocks that followed. Frances' face told the story of her first experience at the evaluation center. She walked into the house sobbing. Her appointment had been with a psychiatric social worker whose job was to take down Michael's case history and test him. She was a gray-haired, dour, stern-faced woman, determined to test Michael at any cost. In the midst of the testing, as she battled against Michael's stubborn desire not to cooperate, Frances asked about Michael's potential. Without batting an eyelash the woman responded, "Can't you see he's retarded?"

The other appointments were the same. The clinic is part of a large county hospital complex in old and often quite dilapidated buildings, with crowded, noisy, dingy corridors and bureaucratic personnel whose personal attitudes seemed to reflect the unattractive surroundings of the hospital.

Frances' second appointment was with a psychologist who spent an hour with Michael, watching him play with toys and taking copious notes. During the whole hour he never once smiled or talked to him or encouraged him in any fashion. The psychologist's only responses to my wife's questions were either grunts or "We'll see." It was not as brutal an appointment as the first one, but it was hardly hopeful.

A neurologist, the head of the evaluation team, was the last to see Michael. He was a change from the first two. He was willing to talk; in fact, he kept up a running commentary during the whole examination. He could also, on occasion, smile. He made a half-hearted attempt to befriend and calm Michael. But his examination was very brief, almost perfunctory. He quickly examined Michael, checked his reflexes, and then, as he walked out of the room, asked my wife if she and I could meet with the staff on the following Wednesday morning for a review of the staff's findings.

On Wednesday we found a number of parents obviously waiting for their appointment with the staff. Each couple would be called by name, walk down a long corridor and into an office. Fifteen, twenty minutes would pass, and then the door would open, the parents would leave, and another family would be called. I sat with Frances on the hard, wooden hospital bench, holding her hand and not saying a word. I had spent a sleepless night, afraid of the neurologist's words, while retaining the slim hope that the final report would contain a hint of comfort and some hope for the future. Now as I sat on the bench, there was nothing for me to say, and I could not pray. I could only sit close to Frances and hold her hand, trying to draw some strength and courage from her presence.

"Agress," the nurse called, and we dutifully trooped down the corridor. I shall always remember my first impression of that consultation room. It was long and narrow, lined on one side with various books and on the other side with some broken toys haphazardly scattered on a shelf. At the front of the room was a table, bare except for a thin folder containing what I assumed was the final evaluation of Michael. The three staff members sat unsmiling behind the desk: the social worker on one side, the psychologist on the other, and the neurologist in the middle.

Walking to the desk, I felt as if I were facing a military

tribunal to hear the result of my court-martial.

The neurologist stood up, greeted us, and asked us to sit down in front of the desk. He then took a paper from the folder, glanced at it, and handed down the verdict. "We've evaluated, tested, and examined Michael and find that he is retarded."

That was it.

"What about the findings at the medical center, the doubts in their minds, the possibility that Michael has an average or above-average intelligence, blocked and distorted by an emotional problem?" I could hear myself almost pleading with the doctor for some crumb of hope, some hesitancy or hedging in his conclusion.

"I've heard that before. Whenever there's something wrong with a child, some doctor says that it has to do with an emotional disturbance. It's just not so. Look at Michael's test score. He tests retarded. Does he talk? Does he play with other children? You have a younger child. Can he do what Steve does?"

All I could do was sit silently, staring at the neurologist. Then Frances asked, "What do we do with Michael? He's five years old. We can't just keep him home. Where do we send him?"

How often were we to repeat those words over the next nine months.

"I can suggest a fine private school for Michael. It's right here in Chicago. This is the address and phone number. Visit them and tell them that I recommended Michael as a student."

The school was on the far north side of Chicago in a residential, treelined neighborhood. Twice we drove around the block before we found it. It was a two-story fortresslike brick building surrounded by a five-foot iron picket fence. It may once have been the home of some wealthy family bent on keeping strangers far from the house or the grounds. As I walked through the open gateway, I could think only of a prison.

Inside we were greeted by a thin, stern-faced woman and a large German shepherd dog. We told the woman, the director of the school, that this school had been recommended to us. "Fine," she said, "I think you will find our school most satisfactory. We teach our boys and girls self-control. They also learn to dress themselves, care for their personal belongings, and ultimately we hope that we can help them acquire certain simple skills such as basket weaving."

We left the school as quickly and politely as we could. Michael was terrified of dogs, and we had no intention of institutionalizing him.

We had had enough of the evaluation clinic, its experts, and their suggestions. We would now strike out on our own.

We had heard of a school under the auspices of the Jewish Family Counseling Service of Chicago, the Virginia Frank School, that dealt with emotionally disturbed children. The director, a very sympathetic woman who spoke with the faintest trace of a Viennese accent, said she would like to help Michael. "However, our school is limited to four- and five-year-olds who have some emotional problems. We hope to work with them so that at the age of six they may be able to enter public school. I'm afraid that Michael's handicaps are too severe for us. I really can't see how we could hope to prepare him for the first grade of public school.

"May I suggest that you visit the Jewish Family Agency," she concluded. "They have a very fine school for retarded children in Chicago. Michael may well benefit from this type of schooling."

This was hardly the answer we had hoped for, but at least Michael would be receiving some education.

The following week we met with a social worker from the agency. Before Michael would be accepted in the school for retarded children, we were required to meet with a staff psychologist. The school felt that it was as important to treat the parents as to educate the child. This seemed sensible to us.

We desperately wanted to know how to deal with Michael and how to handle our own emotions.

The psychologist was kind and considerate, responsive to our fears and growing sense of frustration. He made an appointment for us with the school principal and discussed the requirement that all parents of retarded children meet together with him once a month.

"These meetings help familiarize you with the work that we at the school and the agency do; they also give us an opportunity to learn about you as parents. How do you relate to your child? How does he function in his own environment?"

For the first time in weeks, we left the psychologist's office with some hope for Michael's future, hope that was reinforced when we first walked into the school the following week.

There was no iron fence, and no large dog in the corridor. A group of children walked by with their teacher, smiling and talking to each other. The principal greeted us, led us into her office, and, turning to Michael, said, "Come with me, and we'll go into a class so that you can meet the teacher and play with the children." As she led Michael away, she whispered to us, "I'm taking him into our special observation classroom. We have a window through which we can see the children and they can't see us."

Time passed very slowly—five, ten, fifteen minutes. Finally she returned. "I'm afraid we can't accept him into our school. He's too hyperactive. Why, he didn't play with a toy for more than ten seconds! Our children are placid. He would be a very disruptive influence on them. The teacher would have to spend all her time controlling him.

"No—I'm sorry, he just doesn't fit our program."

The director of the Virginia Frank School had also given us the names of two schools with very small enrollments that specialized in the education and treatment of severely disturbed children.

We called the first one and set up an appointment for two

weeks hence. "I'm sorry," the receptionist said, "the doctor couldn't possibly see you any earlier."

The school was very new: one wing of the building was still under construction. The lobby had the most sterile, antiseptic look I have ever encountered. The walls and ceiling were white, the floor covered with square black and white tiles. The receptionist, who was wearing a white smock, asked us to be seated while she phoned the doctor.

He came out to greet us and asked us to wait in the lobby while he spent some time with Michael in his office. Ten minutes later he invited us in.

"Michael puzzles me," he said. "He may well be retarded, he may have normal intelligence but be deeply disturbed, or he may well be both retarded and emotionally disturbed. I don't know if we can help him. We have a waiting list, and should we agree to accept him, he could not enter before the beginning of next year. Our school is also quite expensive.

"Finally, we have one definite, immovable rule. He must stay with us, and you will not be permitted to visit him for the first year."

How could we send Michael away, even if they did accept him, which did not seem likely? This was no answer.

We called the second school, and the psychiatrist who was also the director spoke to us by phone. He did not think that Michael would fit into his school. Furthermore, he was running out of money and could not be certain that the school would survive past the end of the semester.

For seven months Frances and I searched for help, and in that time we had been told that he was retarded, too handicapped for a class of emotionally disturbed children, too hyperactive for a class of retarded children, and did not fit into the specific intellectual and emotional category of two specialized schools. We had fled the one school willing to accept him because it resembled a jail. I began to have the same nightmarish feelings I had had the day our original pediatrician said, "Michael is brain-damaged."

During these months Michael's behavior had become more erratic. He was more hyperactive, if that were possible, more destructive, more intractable. Frances was desperate. The weekends were bad enough, but at least the family spent some time together. Monday became "Black Monday" to Frances— the start of a new week, when I would be at the temple and she would be home alone with Michael.

And now I started to torture myself with another question: Had I been wrong to leave New York? Had I been selfish to move to Aurora, hoping for some fragment of happiness for Frances and myself without thoroughly planning for Michael's future? Michael had been receiving some help, if only four hours a week. In the Chicago area he had nothing.

Almost as a reflex, we returned to the director of the Virginia Frank School. We had followed her suggestions. What now?

"There is a school," she answered, "but I've hesitated to give you the name. It's a new school, and I've never visited it, nor has it been given any kind of professional evaluation. In fact, some professionals feel that it isn't any good because it isn't selective enough. They will accept *any type* of handicapped child. But all the parents I've met whose children go there have described it in the most glowing terms. You have nothing to lose—you might as well give it a try. The school's name is the Grove School for Exceptional Children, and the director is Mrs. Virginia Matson."

5

The Grove School

Even calling for an appointment at the Grove School was different from our previous experiences.

"Come right over," Virginia Matson replied. "Where do you live? Aurora? Take the Tri-State north, get off at the Deerfield exit—it's the very next exit after you pay a toll—and drive partway through town. You won't miss the street."

And that was that. No conditions. No waiting period. Just "come right over."

That night was a troubled, sleepless one for me. *What will happen,* I thought, *if Michael is refused admittance to the school, or if it's another institution with high walls and a hopeless, jaillike atmosphere? Where will I go from here?* My hopes had been raised too frequently the past seven months, only to be dashed against the rocks of bitter reality. Other promising appointments had evaporated. I was afraid to hope. I really couldn't hope.

The next day, the sun was shining and though it was cold, it was also invigorating. The lawns and trees were covered with white. As a child in New York, I thought snow was dirty gray. In Deerfield this morning, it was clean.

The Grove School was meeting in a church. As I walked into the building, I could easily hear the voices of the children look into the classrooms. I saw spastic children, blind children, a child who could not walk or talk. She had to be carried from her wheelchair into the classroom. She was being taught to crawl. There were hyperactive children and children sitting quietly and attentively in a classroom while the teacher wrote math problems on the blackboard. No classroom had more than six youngsters. One had as few as two.

There were young pretty teachers and middle-aged ones, male and female. All were smiling. All were patient. An aura of love almost literally seemed to emanate from them. Every child was being loved. Every one was doing some work. Every one was being treated as a precious human being.

Virginia Matson came hurrying toward us. If I were to cast a movie about the Grove School, I would select the marvelous British actress Margaret Rutherford to portray Virginia Matson. She does not have Margaret Rutherford's square, jutting jaw or stern, martial appearance, but there is the same unique, strong character, a large, very warm person. There is also the same impression of busyness. She fires her words at you, and if you don't listen carefully, you may not catch them.

"You must be Rabbi Agress," were her first words, "and you're Mrs. Agress." Looking down at our two sons, she continued, "Which one is Michael? . . . Come, Michael, do you want to come into the classroom? The teacher's name is Mrs. Clayton . . . Mrs. Clayton, this is Michael . . . Michael, make yourself comfortable."

We hustled along to keep up with Virginia Matson.

"Now, Agresses—do you want some coffee while we talk in the kitchen? We use the kitchen as our office. It's cold outside, and I'm sure you'll join me for some coffee."

We ran after her into the kitchen, and stood there dazed while she poured coffee for the three of us. Did she really mean Michael was accepted? What about testing him, watching him interact with other children?

"Of course he's admitted. Do you want to leave him here for

today or do you want to start tomorrow?"

That was it. We could barely believe our ears. Not only was Michael going to school, but it was a beautiful, tender, loving school.

"Now about the tuition," Mrs. Matson continued, "our costs are $750 per child. But I know what rabbis make, so that whatever you feel that you can pay will be fine with the school. Perhaps the Aurora school system could pay towards Michael's tuition, since he cannot attend there. This has been done for a number of our children."

(Our local board of education eventually voted to send the Grove School the equivalent of educating a child in Aurora, at that time approximately five hundred fifty dollars.)

A half-hour later we prepared to leave. Michael didn't want to go. He was busy touching the toys and smiling at his new teacher. We hadn't seen him smile in weeks.

Somehow, everything I thought to say to Virginia Matson seemed wholly inadequate. I said, "Thank you, and God bless you," and left.

The ride home was silent. I choked back the tears as I drove. At that time, I still thought it unmanly to cry. My thoughts were whirling. Was this the end of one phase in my life and the beginning of a new one? Could I allow myself once again to hope and believe? What fate had brought me this morning to the Grove School and introduced me to this unusual woman?

We arrived home at noon. We had left Aurora at eight-thirty, and now a brief 3½ hours later our lives were changed.

I sat down for lunch and still could not find the words to express my feelings. After eating, I put on my hat and coat and drove to the temple. I walked in, went immediately to the small chapel, opened the ark door, kissed the Torah mantel, whispered, "Thank You, Lord," and cried. I had come home.

The 116th Psalm is recited in the synagogue on Jewish holidays as part of the *Hallel* ("thanksgiving") service. I had often read the psalm automatically but now it had acquired a meaning for me.

I love that the Lord should hear
My voice and my supplications.
Because He hath inclined His ear unto me,
Therefore will I call upon Him all my days.

The cords of death compassed me,
And the straits of the nether-world got hold upon me;
I found trouble and sorrow.
But I called upon the name of the Lord:
"I beseech Thee, O Lord, deliver my soul."
Gracious is the Lord, and righteous;
Yea, our God is compassionate.
The Lord preserveth the simple;
I was brought low, and He saved me.

Return, O my soul, unto thy rest;
For the Lord hath dealt bountifully with thee.
For Thou has delivered my soul from death,
Mine eyes from tears,
And my feet from stumbling.
I shall walk before the Lord
In the lands of the living.

Psalms 116:1-9

6

A New Day

Mike awoke early, couldn't wait to get dressed, barely ate his breakfast, and ran to the car. His time at the Grove School the day before had been so enjoyable he wanted more.

So began our daily trek to Deerfield—fifty miles northeast. In addition, I had to be at the University of Chicago on the city's south side two days a week. So I began driving the two sides of a huge triangle, arriving in Deerfield by nine o'clock each morning, then heading back down Edens Expressway to my class at ten-thirty. In the afternoon it was back to Deerfield, then home to Aurora. Totals for the day: 200 miles, $2.40 in tolls.

The other three days of the week Frances drove.

When I had no studying to do, I would sometimes arrive at the Grove School an hour or so before classes let out and spend the time watching the children play on the grass, occasionally peeking into Mike's room (any parent could sit in on a class), or when Mrs. Matson wasn't too busy, chatting with her.

She had started the school in response to an appeal from a desperate pair of parents much like us. She first met their seemingly uneducable Peter on Saturday, November 1, 1958. (Frances and I were astonished when we learned this—we were married on the very next day, Sunday, November 2, 1958, in a

55

Chicago hotel. A Jewish sage wrote that "God in His infinite mercy produces the cure before He brings an illness into the world." At the very moment we were standing under the wedding canopy, He was preparing the salvation, the Grove School, for our trial.)

Virginia's initial plan had been to work with Peter one hour every Saturday morning while she continued with her regular duties as a teacher, housewife, mother of five children, and author. But, in her oft-repeated words, "The Lord had other work for me." She soon acquired a second pupil who needed her unique talents, and within two years, four more severely handicapped children. As she has noted in her beautifully written and poignant book *A School for Peter*, the state educational bureaucracy constantly fought her. It was a time of God's testing.

The day Michael began, the Grove School was educating fifty handicapped children ranging from the bright youngster with some brain dysfunction and emotional problems to multihandicapped children unable to walk, speak, or even toilet-train themselves.

As I watched them—a few in the advanced class sitting at their desks doing math problems, others such as Michael spelling out words and recognizing letters through the use of a flannelboard, the most severely handicapped crawling about a cross-pattern to develop their motor skills—I was once again struck by the unique atmosphere of the school. Though the ages and backgrounds of the teachers varied widely, all seemed to possess great care, love, and devotion for their young charges. The day-to-day operation of the school was in the very capable hands of Mrs. Wright, a slim, attractive, gray-haired woman who with gentle yet firm words guided the staff, answered the anxious questions of parents, and served as confidant to all. The office was run by Mrs. Elickson, ever smiling, always prepared to help with financial problems about state, county, or community aid. Mrs. Clayton was Michael's teacher, a strikingly lovely young woman, poised, calm, cheerful, aware of the emotional needs of each of her pupils, dispensing discipline firmly yet lovingly.

Overall control and direction lay in the hands of Virginia Matson. The highly unusual atmosphere of the school, its sense of purpose and idealism, the aura of love that enveloped it had been instilled by her. The school is an extension of her personality. Virginia, in turn, has been molded by her faith. She is a devout Christian who daily lives by Christian tenets. She came to her belief through a process of questioning, doubting, and being tested. Her first child, a lovely girl, was born with a cleft palate. Her strength and courage during the child's first years, the suspense of surgery on the palate, and the daily speech therapy which finally culminated in complete success as the little girl overcame her handicap served to solidify Virginia's awareness of God's loving-kindness. The deepest, most abiding faith belongs to those who have, like Jacob, "wrestled with the angel"—questioning, suffering, and coming through the crucible of fire spiritually whole.

For Virginia, God is everywhere; His will can be found in all of man's actions. He speaks with "a still, small voice," but if one tries one can hear the Voice quite clearly. Her meeting with Peter's parents on that fateful Saturday morning in November, 1958, was not a chance visit, though she had initially come to discuss Peter's older brother John, who was then one of her students. Rather she was to see it as a call from the Almighty that set off a good deal of struggle within her. She was like Jeremiah, who questioned God when first called to His service—"Then I said, 'Ah, Lord God! Behold I cannot speak; for I am a child' " (Jeremiah 1:6). Was working with Peter going to take too much time away from her other duties? Above all, was she capable of teaching such a child? Eventually, her response was like Jeremiah's; she heeded the Voice.

Her trust in His bounty and providence is total. *She must be a saint*, I thought after she'd offered to adjust the tuition for us that first day. *How does she expect the school to run? There are probably other parents sending children who have as little*

57

money as we do. I am now certain that had I voiced my doubts she would have answered, "You needn't worry. God will provide." She does not sit back and wait for manna from heaven. No! She scrounges for every dollar she can obtain for the school; she pleads with local school boards and the Illinois Department of Education, contributes all royalties from the sale of her books, wheedles money from various foundations. But when a crisis arises and the Grove School is in danger, she places her complete trust in God that He will not let her and her "little angels" down.

The term, to her, is not a euphemism. She literally believes that her youngsters—deformed, crippled, disturbed, handicapped, maimed in body and mind, but with pure, innocent hearts and believing souls—are closer to the Lord than any other of His creatures. "Blessed are they that mourn: for they shall be comforted. Blessed are the meek: for they shall inherit the earth. Blessed are the pure in heart: for they shall see God." (Matthew 5:4—*King James Version*) These children have been given as a challenge, an opportunity for parents and teacher to grow spiritually. No one who has seen a palsied child slowly, torturously, move one leg and then another in an attempt to walk a few steps, or the autistic youngster struggle to break out of his imprisonment of silence, can ever doubt the almost superhuman will and courage of these little angels. The parent who seizes this challenge and grows with it soon learns the true blessings these children bring with them. Virginia Matson lives by this principle and tries gently and kindly to instill it in her staff and the parents.

This guiding concept has led her to accept any handicapped child, no matter how severely impaired. I recall the warning Frances and I heard when we were first told of the Grove School: "Some professionals feel it isn't any good because it isn't selective enough. They will accept any type of handicapped child." Most of Virginia's problems and battles with the bureaucracy and so-called special-education experts, most of the attempts to close her school were due to her insistence that all handicapped children be accepted. She feels that *every* child can be helped, and every one deserves the opportunity to develop to the highest level of his potential. The greater the challenge, the greater the reward and the blessing. By charting and studying the progress of each child, we can learn lessons that will benefit all children regardless of the seeming disparate nature of their brain dysfunctions and multiple afflictions.

One of the crucial needs of all the children, Virginia soon learned, was to bring a sense of order into their young lives. The child with a brain dysfunction receives impressions of the outside world totally different from what a normal person receives. Though he may have normal hearing, the sounds coming into his brain are jumbled or have an entirely different meaning. His eyes see, yet they do not see; they send distorted messages to the brain. His world is not the ordered world of the normal person. For years educators could not understand why some bright children had such trouble reading, sometimes reversing the order of words or letters. We now realize that this is usually a symptom of a brain dysfunction, of crossed signals in the mind. With proper training these can be modified or completely corrected. All these children, in particular the more seriously handicapped, must have order, a tightly structured learning environment, so that they may begin to sense some order in their hitherto chaotic existence.

Virginia realized the need for order by working with such children as Peter, by taking courses with scholars in the field of special education, and by visiting institutions in other parts of the world that were doing pioneer work in this area. But I believe that Virginia's spiritual ideas also played a part. God in His infinite wisdom created a perfect world, bringing order out of chaos. "In the beginning God created the heaven and the earth. Now the earth was unformed and void . . . . and God saw every thing that He had made, and behold, it was very good" (Genesis 1:1-2, 31).

Adam, the prototype of man, by a perverse and rebellious

deed, altered this perfect world and reintroduced chaos. To restore order is, therefore, a continuation of the Lord's work, a sharing in His act of creation and forgiveness. As Virginia worked slowly and painstakingly, first with Peter, then with Mary, and then with four other children, was she not helping to bring new life, through order, to these children? Was she not acting in the most spiritual sense possible?

From the very first Virginia asked me to bring the Jewish festival of Chanukah to the children. As she explained to me, "Our Jewish children should not feel left out during the Christmas season. Since Chanukah usually falls during the same month, why don't you teach all of our children about this happy holiday?" Every year since 1965 I have gone to the school to celebrate this festival with the children—except once when, because of a snowstorm, I couldn't get there. So I came later for another marvelous Jewish festival, ideal for children: Purim.

They loved the story of the holiday as told in the biblical book of Esther, how beautiful Queen Esther and kindly Mordecai foiled the plans of villainous Haman. I brought along the special noisemakers called groggers which we give our own children at the temple, and I distributed them to the Grove School children. I told them to use their groggers whenever I came to the name of Haman in my story just as Jewish children and adults do on Purim when the *megillah* ("scroll") of Esther is read at temple. It was a noisy Purim afternoon at the Grove School, but how the children enjoyed themselves! And how they loved the *hamantashen*, the specially baked three-cornered tarts they ate after listening to the story and singing the songs about Purim.

As I left they shouted, "Thanks—hope to see you next year." These words, together with their smiles and laughter, were more payment than I have ever received for conducting a religious service.

"I want these children to come into contact with people of a different faith, to learn about other religions," Virginia said to me after one of my sessions, "You may not think it, but every one of them, no matter how handicapped, learns something from you. They want to feel God's presence near them. He comforts them and gives them the courage to go on living and learning to overcome their handicaps." Many a time Virginia has seen these severely brain-damaged, hyperactive children grow calm and even serene while listening to an old Christian hymn.

The school's most vital attribute of all is what I call its "aura of love." So strong is this love that it seems literally to hang in the air. I felt it the first day I walked in, and I experience it even more strongly every time I return to visit Virginia and the children.

The brain-damaged child must have love in order to function. Unfortunately, because of his handicap, hyperactivity, inability to express himself, and his distorted view of the world, he cannot express his love and in fact seems to reject the love others offer him.

Virginia was determined to bring these little ones love. The Grove School staff is a widely disparate group, varying greatly in age and educational background. They need not have taken graduate courses in special education nor even have a degree in education. But they all love their handicapped students and are able to communicate this feeling to the children. It would seem self-evident that special-education teachers, psychologists, therapists, or social workers dealing with the handicapped should be devoted to them. However, that is not always the case—these youngsters can come to be viewed as objects to be studied, diagnosed, analyzed, and categorized, or as x number of case studies to be investigated. Virginia selects for her staff only those who love her little angels and who have a passionate desire to help them.

The emphasis on love is therapeutically sound. It produces results, in some cases almost miraculous ones. But to Virginia, love is not only medicine to help confused minds. It is the essence of life itself, the motivating force behind all that is good and decent. God is present everywhere and can be encountered at any time, but only if love is in the person's heart. God is approached through love, love for Him and for His creations. The highest expression of love for Virginia is in her relation to her angels, the beautiful, innocent, injured children at the Grove School.

Judaism has traditionally attached great importance to the ties of love between parent and offspring. "Honor thy father and thy mother" was but the cornerstone of many such commandments. Love of parents was second only to the love of God, and obligations flowed both ways, for love must come from parent to child as well as from child to parent. I knew this; I thought that as a son, husband, and father I was fulfilling these injunctions. But it was Virginia Matson who helped me understand their ultimate significance and true meaning in Michael's life.

As an infant Michael resisted being held and showed no delight when either Frances or I kissed him. During the first month of his life, he cried for an hour to an hour and a half each day; nothing we did, neither holding, nor fondling, nor caressing did any good. Then he outgrew that to become a cheerful baby, always smiling or laughing. However, he smiled at everyone, making no distinction between family or stranger. He exhibited no sign of sibling rivalry when Steve was born. He ignored the baby, had no interest in touching or feeding him, and didn't try to distract Frances when she fed him. His indifference disturbed us, but we assumed that every child is different and that he would change.

When we learned of Mike's brain damage, we realized his rejection, his hatred of being held or kissed, was a symptom of his handicap. He became more hyperactive and destructive, no longer the laughing baby but a morose, afflicted child more animal than human.

I had to contend with my own emotions. Learning about Michael's handicap had set off within me waves of self-destructive reactions that fed upon each other. I was trapped in a vicious cycle. I felt helpless and hopeless, alone, ashamed of Michael and of myself, and I felt guilty because I was ashamed. Shakespeare wrote, "Better it were, that all the miseries which nature owns were ours at once, than guilt." At times I hated myself as well as Michael, whom I thought of as the cause of all my sorrow and the destroyer of my dreams. I loathed myself, and I overcompensated by not punishing Michael regardless of what he did. Needless to say, my almost schizophrenic treatment—hatred one moment and overindulgence the next—added to his confusion and made him more hyperactive and unhappy.

Michael had never said a word on his own. When he was a year old we could get him to repeat "mama" or "papa" when we urged him by saying, "Michael, say 'mama.'" But he never said anything of his own volition. Even his prompted speaking stopped when he was 2½ years old. One of my greatest fears was that I would never hear him speak. I had a recurring dream in which Michael would run to me and move his lips, but I heard nothing.

We had his hearing tested and, as we had anticipated, there was nothing physically wrong.

"Will my son speak?" I asked the pediatric neurologist after Michael had been examined at the Einstein Medical Center.

"I don't know," he answered. "Physically, there seems to be nothing holding him back. However, even if his problem is largely emotional, this doesn't mean that he will ultimately talk. These children are the most difficult to treat. There is no way that you can force him. Just talk and read to him as you would to a normal child, and let's hope for the best."

The supervisor at the nursery school in New York took an entirely different approach. "Since you do everything for him without his asking for it," she said, "there's no reason for him to talk. Try ignoring him when he points and keep telling him that you won't do anything unless he asks for it."

The suggestion made sense to us, but it didn't work. Either Michael would give up after pointing for a while or he would scream, cry, and throw a tantrum until we relented.

We sensed a change in Michael as soon as he entered the Grove School. It had an immediate calming effect upon him. He obviously enjoyed going to a school and he wasn't as destructive at home. He didn't have as many tantrums, nor did he cry or bang his head against the wall as often.

"Mrs. Matson, please tell me the truth—do you think Michael will ever speak?" I asked a few days after he had started attending.

"Rabbi, our prognosis has to be very guarded," she replied. "He has some very grave auditory and sensory perception problems. He may either be suffering from aphasia—that is, he hears, but the sound symbols do not convey any meaning to him—or else he hears garbled or confused sound because the two sides of the brain and his two ears do not hear sound simultaneously. Either way, he doesn't hear what we do." This was the first time anyone had explained this to me.

"When you or Frances speak to him," she continued, "try to use the most direct, unambiguous words possible. If you find that certain instructions haven't got through to him, use a different phrase. As the world becomes a little less confusing to him and as he gains some confidence in himself, you should see changes in his behavior. We shall be working with him at school, encouraging him, drawing him out, and having him take at least an hour a day of speech therapy. God is good . . . and Mike is such a lovable child . . . ." Letting the sentence trail off without a conclusion, she looked at me with such understanding, compassion, and belief that a feeling of hope surged through me.

The weeks flew quickly by. Spring had finally arrived, and the small community of Deerfield looked lovely with the green lawns, blossoming flowers, and budding trees. Michael was changing, too. He would dash into school, run over to Mrs. Clayton with a broad, welcoming smile, and then dash over to play with one of the toys in the room. He also had a set routine when he came home. He would toss his coat down and rush to the refrigerator for something to eat or drink.

One day, approximately a month after he had started school, he came running into the kitchen, opened the refrigerator, turned to his mother, pointed and said it loud and clear: "Pop!" We couldn't believe our ears. Had we heard correctly? With an attempt at nonchalance, Frances said, "What did you say, Michael?"

And he repeated, "Pop."

We hugged and kissed him and told him how happy we were to hear him ask for something and that we wanted him to continue. Frances and I looked at each other with tears in our eyes and a prayer of thanksgiving in our hearts.

I think of that occasion as a miracle, God showing His love to us, just as I shall always think of the moment when I first heard about the Grove School as providential.

There were a number of ingredients in this miracle. The Grove School had a calming effect upon Michael. It had also influenced my own attitude toward my son. The situation no longer seemed so hopeless. I wasn't as despondent or angry at Michael, and, of course, this affected him. His teacher and speech therapist had worked diligently with him. Above all, the love he felt in class and at home had bolstered his confidence and had encouraged him to open up and communicate with those around him. My wish had come true. Michael had spoken.

As days passed he expanded his limited vocabulary. He would awaken us a half-hour or an hour before the alarm rang by rushing into our bedroom and shouting, "Time! Time!" This little boy who had seemed impervious to love, who had resisted all our attempts to hug and kiss him, now showed himself as a warmly affectionate child. He eventually would walk up to his brother and sister and kiss them. More than one Saturday (the one day in the week Frances tried to sleep late) Michael tiptoed into our bedroom, bent down to his mother, kissed her gently on the forehead and whispered, "Mommy, is it time to get up yet?"

The great philosopher Martin Buber once wrote, "He who loves, brings God and the world together." I could now feel God's presence in the work of the Grove School, in the joy on all the children's faces, in the love my child felt for me, and finally in the fact that I could reciprocate, that I could love Michael in return.

Reflections—Part One

7
Shame

Why was I ashamed of my handicapped child? At first I didn't even realize it. I lived in such a state of shock, was so emotionally dead, that I avoided all contact with friends or acquaintances. But as the initial numbness wore off, I found that I still could not talk about Michael or his condition to anyone. I avoided calling my dearest friends for fear that they might ask me about my family, and I would either have to answer evasively or tell an outright lie.

I was to learn at our first meeting with Grove School parents that many others with brain-damaged or retarded children have the same feelings. All the parents, together with our children, were invited to the newly acquired property in Lake Forest, Illinois, for a picnic on the lawn one Sunday afternoon in July.

The day was pleasantly cool, a breeze coming in from Lake Michigan. The grounds were breath-taking. The buildings were set in the woods a hundred feet off Old Mill Road. There was such a sense of pastoral calm and serenity in the air that even Michael was noticeably calmer.

Mrs. Matson explained that the property had formerly belonged to the Ridge Farm and was a residential home for pretubercular girls. She guided us through the three buildings being converted into classrooms and offices and showed us the largest room, which would serve as a combination gym, lunchroom, and assembly hall. A clearing in back of the farthest house was to become an outdoor playground, and a narrow dirt path would be ideal for a nature walk.

Perhaps it was due to the loveliness of the evening and the beauty of the school's natural setting, or perhaps it was the sight of the parents walking slowly with their handicapped children or, in a number of situations, pushing wheelchairs. In any case, I found myself easily chatting to another father, discussing our children, the frustrations in finding a good school for them, and the almost total adulation we felt toward Virginia Matson and her staff. For the first time I discovered that I could talk about Michael without feeling anxious or uncertain. I also discovered that other parents were hesitant and ashamed of their handicapped children. Just as I, they too, experienced feelings of deep guilt because they felt ashamed.

Shame and guilt quite frequently march hand in hand, setting off a vicious emotional chain reaction and cycle. At first we may deny feeling this emotion or attempt to bury it in the subconscious. However, it will not remain buried, nor can we continue lying to ourselves. Guilt follows shame. What right do we have to blame our innocent child for his affliction? How dare we be ashamed of him? We end this emotional binge by hating ourselves and perhaps subconsciously hating the child who made us feel guilty.

I have known parents who denied that anything was wrong with their youngster out of a deep-rooted sense of shame, depriving these children of necessary medical and psychological attention. The scientific study of mental retardation, brain damage, and perceptual disabilities may be in its infancy, but new discoveries and advancements in treatment are made every day. There is growing hope for these children. To deprive them of treatment is to deny them any hope for the future. Yet this is one of the tragic consequences of an uncontrolled feeling of shame.

Finally, a feeling of shame may do incalculable harm to the self-esteem of the afflicted youngster. This child is often ultrasensitive to every nuance of our emotions. He knows when we are ashamed of him though we may try to hide this feeling from him and ourselves. The handicapped child will go through life facing the indifference and at times outright hostility of others. Children can be so very cruel even when they don't mean to be, calling him "retarded," "slow," "stupid." He will find difficulty in making friends because he is different; others know he is different. He is timid and afraid to try anything new because he finds it so difficult to perform any new task. He will place a low evaluation upon his own abilities because others downgrade him; indeed, our society puts a high premium upon technological skills and intellectual attainments.

We, as parents, can do much in helping build a sense of self-worth. But how are we to do this if we are ashamed of him—and he knows we are ashamed?

One possible solution would be to alter society's attitude toward the handicapped. Some progress has been made toward this. The federal government, starting with the Kennedy administration, has taken a more active role in financing studies in mental retardation, perceptual disabilities, and prenatal care for mothers. Perhaps because of President Kennedy's personal concern with mental retardation (the oldest Kennedy sister is retarded), the American public has become more aware of the magnitude of the problem. State and local agencies are trying to encourage employers to hire the handicapped. Most heartening of all, we are starting to utilize the most modern physiological and psychological techniques in the education and development of the brain-damaged child.

However, the public generally continues to look at the brain-damaged, retarded child in the same old stereotyped way, and our study of the mind is in its infancy.

If I were ever to overcome my feelings of shame concerning

Michael, I had to turn into myself and use my own resources for a solution. I had to consciously accept the fact that I was ashamed and to see that a good deal of my actions and evasions were based upon this feeling. I had to understand the mechanics of shame and use the moral weapons of my faith to combat and triumph over this destructive emotion.

Shame can be a two-edged sword working for our good or ill. All our emotions function in the same manner including diverse ones: hate, anger, ambition. In Ecclesiastes it is written, "I considered all labor and all excelling in work, that it is a man's rivalry with his neighbor." A Jewish sage interpreted the biblical verse found in Genesis, "And God saw everything that He had made, and behold, it was very good," in the following manner, "Behold, it was very good—that is, the will to evil. But is the will to evil good? That is astonishing! Yet were it not for the will to evil, men would not build homes, or take wives, or propagate, or engage in business."

Shame alerts us to the fact that we have done something wrong. It presupposes a certain degree of maturity, knowledge, and an awareness of our actions; the very young, or the very feeble-minded, know no shame. When man first sinned, he learned shame. Adam and Eve, after they had eaten from the tree of knowledge, covered their nakedness with fig leaves and hid themselves from God out of a sense of shame. The immoral person is one who has lost all his capacity for shame. Henry Wadsworth Longfellow, in his poem "The Ladder of Saint Augustine," wrote:

St. Augustine! Well hast thou said,
That of our vices we can frame
A ladder, if we will but tread
Beneath our feet each deed of shame.

Shame, on the other hand, can be misdirected and cause us a good deal of harm. We may be ashamed of felt shortcomings based upon values in our society having nothing to do with our inherent worth. For example, we live in a cosmetic culture that places a great premium upon physical beauty. We hold Miss and Mrs. America beauty pageants and even contests for the prettiest teen-ager and baby. Our children's heroes are the Hollywood stars and starlets. What of the ugly child? To paraphrase Abraham Lincoln, "God must have loved the ugly. He made so many of them." To be ugly is to be a source of shame and even derision. I've heard of a high-school contest to elect the ugliest boy and girl in the school. What a cruel jest! How harmful it must be to the psychological development of those in the most formative of their years.

Shame may also come from misplaced pride and self-importance, our desire to be perfect. This wish would be quite laudable if we thought in terms of moral perfection, but we leave that realm to the saint. Our bent toward perfection is more egotistical, founded upon material measurements that have nothing at all to do with honesty or decency.

Only fifty years ago we were ashamed of such physical illnesses as tuberculosis or cancer. We are still ashamed of mental illness. We no longer lock our insane away in hidden rooms as did the fictional Rochester in Charlotte Bronte's *Jane Eyre,* though we tolerate mental hospitals that are a throwback to the medieval bedlams. But we hide the fact that someone in our family may have had a nervous breakdown or is seeing a psychiatrist. We call the psychiatrist a "headshrinker" and the mental hospital is a "booby hatch."

Children are frequently ashamed of illness. For a few years our younger son Steve didn't want us to tell anyone when he was sick and would become almost hysterical at the thought that his friends might find out. As he grows older and more mature, he has learned to accept colds, fever, and flu without feeling personally responsible and less than perfect. We all grow older, but we don't all mature, and the shame of being sick frequently continues well into adulthood.

This same willfully misplaced urge for ego-building perfection can poison our relationship with our children. We think of our children as extensions of ourselves. They resemble us, inherit or acquire many of our personality traits. Our sons carry on the family name long after we are gone.

And so we make demands of our children that may far exceed their ability to produce. How often have I been told by parents that they cannot understand why their child is receiving such poor grades in school. It's the teacher's fault or the school curriculum, but never their youngster. They so want their child to be accepted at college that they ignore their child's intellectual limitations and permanently harm his future growth and development.

All too frequently we burden our children with our own unfulfilled dreams and hopes of glory, power, prestige, and accomplishments. We dream of the day when they will make us proud. If they do not live up to our great expectations, we express our disappointment. The waiting rooms of psychiatrists' offices are filled with adults obsessed by a compulsion to please their parents regardless of the consequences.

A number of years ago a father asked me to help him with his teen-age daughter. She had taken to smoking pot, been caught shoplifting, had attempted suicide, and had finally become pregnant. Both in deed and word she was desperately crying out for help, but all her father felt was an overwhelming sense of shame. How could he face his friends with a pregnant fifteen-year-old girl at home! This poor, unfortunate child needed understanding, compassion, and above all, love. Her father gave her scorn, abuse, recrimination, and hate.

I sometimes wonder whether God did not have this in mind when He said, "I the Lord thy God am a jealous God, visiting the iniquity of the fathers upon the children unto the third and fourth generation of them that hate me." The sins visited upon our children may well be our own sins of egotism, vaulting ambition, and selfish arrogance. Their punishment is to live the life of a neurotic, unsatisfied, and unloved adult.

My own feeling of shame was compounded by my upbringing, by the inordinate emphasis placed upon intelligence, learning, and intellectual attainments. Judaism has always stressed learning as a vital part of faith. "Thou shalt teach them [the words of the Bible] diligently to thy children . . .," a verse found in Deuteronomy 6:7, is part of the *Shema,* the most important prayer in our service. My father was a rabbi, my maternal grandfather a scribe, a scholarly devout Jew who spent his lifetime studying the Talmud and lovingly transcribing the Torah scrolls by hand with a quill pen. Coincidently, Frances' maternal grandfather was also a scribe, for years the only scribe in Chicago. When Michael was born, I took for granted the fact that he would go to college. The pediatrician's few words, "Your son is brain-damaged," effectively shattered that notion. Not only would he not go to college, but I didn't know whether he would ever read a book, write a sentence, or even say a word. I have been told by special-education teachers, who work with the retarded, that parents with a college education find it the most difficult raising a slow or retarded child.

Years passed before I could finally say that I was no longer ashamed.

My meeting with parents of handicapped children at the Grove School helped. I wasn't the only father ashamed of his child, and so I didn't need to feel quite so guilty. Michael's personality began to break through the wall he had erected to protect himself, and I began to understand and appreciate this truly unique child.

Finally, my ideas, sense of values, my whole personality changed. Suffering had altered me. I became aware of my frailties, my inadequacies, my dependence upon others and ultimately upon God. I learned that society's norms and standards of excellence are not necessarily meaningful to me and may clash with eternal moral values. I could understand what I had been and appreciate what I had become.

Humility is, of course, a cornerstone of Judaism and Christianity. The prophet Micah preaches, "It hath been told thee, O man, what is good, and what the Lord doth require of thee:

Only to do justly, and to love mercy, and to walk humbly with thy God."

St. Augustine writes: "It is pride that changed angels into devils; and it is humility that makes men as angels." God accords Moses His highest accolade when the Bible refers to him as "very humble above all men." And Jesus proclaims, "For every one that exalteth himself shall be abased; and he that humbleth himself shall be exalted.

Although I had studied the Bible, including Micah, and I could appreciate this virtue in others, only Michael's tragedy could force me to see how important it was for me.

But a word of caution about humility. It has at times become synonymous with groveling self-abasement, an image of a man walking with head hung low, bent over, eyes cast to the ground, meek and afraid. *Webster's Intercollegiate Dictionary* notes that "in current loose use, *humble* implies undue self-depreciation, and meek spiritlessness and timid submissiveness." Humility of this nature is more vice than virtue. Or it may serve to cloak mediocrity and serve the ugly needs of the hypocrite. Uriah Heep, in Charles Dickens' classic *David Copperfield,* proclaims himself in the midst of his villainy "an 'umble person."

I like to think that the truly humble person is the fortunate individual who is genuinely satisfied with his lifework while accepting his limitations; he is at peace both with himself and the world around him.

I recall with a good deal of affection a college teacher I had who was respected and loved by all his students. He is a scholar in his chosen field of study, has written a number of books, and continues to publish fine works of scholarship. He is a marvelous lecturer who is able to impart to his students a passion for learning and keen knowledge of the subject. Yet above all else I shall remember him for his character. He always spoke gently, never became impatient at students' questions, no matter how inane, and would himself walk to the door or window if he wanted it opened or closed rather than ask any of his students to do it. The nobility of his personality, the gentleness of his soul, and his deep humility were manifest in all his varied actions. He taught me as much about goodness as he did about history. He had no need to boast of his scholarship and achievements nor to bolster his ego with bloated pride and self-praise. Humility came to him out of a sense of self-awareness and human dignity, respect both for himself and for others.

How often have I wished that I could have had the opportunity to share my troubles with him and to ask him for advice. What would his response have been to a handicapped child? I knew he had suffered during his lifetime. He was forced to flee his position as a professor in a leading German university when Hitler became chancellor. I am sure he would have undergone a great deal of anguish at the knowledge that his son was handicapped. But I am equally certain he would have felt no shame.

8
Loneliness

A number of times I have been lonely, but I never felt that frightening sense of being totally alone, isolated in an unreal and nightmarish world, as I did those first few years after Frances and I were told that Michael was brain-damaged.

As an only child I had learned quite early in life the meaning of loneliness. I had wonderfully loving parents, but despite all the attention they gave me, our relationship could never serve as substitute for the companionship of brothers and sisters. I don't mean to imply that my childhood was a period of unalloyed loneliness. I had my friends. I had my books. I loved to spend hours in the public library reading boyhood adventure stories: *Tom Sawyer*, *Huckleberry Finn*, *Penrod*, and the biographies of famous people. I had a vivid imagination that dotted my youth with imaginary friends and heroic escapades. But there were times, especially during summer vacation when I had no school and my friends had gone off with their parents, that I felt the deeply pervasive sadness of solitude.

I went to college and was very fortunate in finding two fine roommates. Both had been born in Europe, spent their formative years in Hitler's concentration camps, lost their immediate families—parents, brothers, sisters—in the inferno of the crematoriums, and now lived with American cousins whom they had found after the war. Isaac was the older of the two: thin, brilliant, occasionally impatient with us. At times he would awaken in the middle of the night after a nightmare, shivering and sweating as if suffering from malaria. David was shorter, with a round face and marvelous disposition. When he smiled (and he smiled very frequently), he looked like a cherub. I cannot remember one instance when he became angry, but at times he could be quite sad. They rarely spoke of their hellish experiences, although David once told me that toward the end of his concentration-camp days he kept warm by covering himself with the lifeless bodies of fellow inmates. Both David and Isaac were more dead than alive when the Allied armies finally liberated them.

During our years as students at the theological seminary we became close friends. We spent hours discussing our hopes for the future and our philosophies of life. I shall always cherish the memory of those days, the feeling of togetherness, our lengthy conversations, and our close friendships; during those years my sense of loneliness was set aside by the companionship I was able to build.

Young men entering the rabbinate are encouraged to get married before they accept an assignment to a congregation. I soon learned why. I was single when I completed my postgraduate education and was ordained. My theological seminary asked me, as a favor, to accept a position in Toronto with a congregation that at the time did not even exist. It was in a newly developed suburban area to which a number of young Jewish couples were moving. A few of these families had requested help from the seminary in creating a synagogue and a religious school for their children. In all likelihood, a large number of Jews would eventually be moving into the area.

The fact that I was young, single, and could live on a very small salary made me a prime candidate for the job. I started from scratch. With the help of the development contractor, I found a house we could use for our worship services. I rented a room with a family and walked from door to door, for at that time I had no car, meeting the Jewish families in the neighborhood, introducing myself, and asking them to join me in building a Jewish congregation. Together with another young man I started a religious school where I served as both principal and teacher. It was extremely hard, slow, tedious work, but gratifyingly successful in the end. Within a few months I had started a congregation, held services every Saturday, and had a religious school enrollment of seventy-five children.

However, I was very lonely. My family and friends were some eight hundred miles away. I always enjoyed meeting people and being with them. Though I have a knack for remembering names and putting people at ease, I find it difficult to form new and close friendships. The families I met in Toronto were quite nice and very hospitable, yet they were no substitute for friends and family. As a single man in a distant city I found myself homesick and lonely; after having done the initial spadework I asked to be reassigned to a pulpit much closer to home. I also felt that the congregation would be better served by a rabbi who was married and would, therefore, be prepared to sink his roots into the community.

I left Toronto in June. The following July I met Frances, and a year and a half later we were married.

For the first time in my life I knew the marvelous all-embracing feeling of total joy. I was engrossed in my work, proud of my congregation and its newly completed synagogue. I had formed close friendships with a number of my congregants. The apartment Frances and I rented, though small, was attractive and our very own. Above all I was married to the most beautiful, loving wife in the world, and I need never feel alone again.

Michael's birth, followed some twenty months later by Stephen's, only added to my sense of happiness and good fortune.

Four happy, contented years passed before Michael was diagnosed as brain-damaged and quite possibly retarded. The first week after our visit to the doctor I saw no one except for my secretary and the few congregants who attended daily services. On Saturday morning I even found an excuse not to deliver a sermon.

I recall as vividly as if it were yesterday the day Frances took Michael to the neurologist. He would either confirm or dismiss our pediatrician's suspicions. I stayed home with Stephen and opened the book that had for ages comforted and consoled those who, like me, were heartsick, frightened, and desolated: the Psalms. I repeated over and over the first few verses of Psalm 6,

O Lord, rebuke me not in Thine anger,
Neither chasten me in Thy wrath.
Be gracious unto me, O Lord, for I languish away;
Heal me, O Lord, for my bones are affrighted.
My soul also is sore affrighted;
And Thou, O Lord, how long?

Return, O Lord, deliver my soul;
Save me for Thy mercy's sake.

And I would cry softly after each reading. There is an old Jewish tradition that in the case of great danger or a grave illness the psalm corresponding to the name of the endangered individual is read. Each letter of the Hebrew alphabet stands for a different number, and so I read various psalms, each chapter bearing on a letter of Michael's Hebrew name.

But to no avail. The neurologist agreed with our pediatrician. In place of unreasoning fear and anxiety, I now felt black despair. A terrifying sense of loneliness came over me as I have never known before, and I pray that I shall never know it again. I had no one to turn to, no one who could help me break out of my self-imposed shell of isolation. I was as bereft as Coleridge's ancient mariner: "Alone, alone all all alone, alone on a wide, wide sea."

Frances tried with all her love and power to rupture the barrier I had erected between myself and the outside world, but with little success. I kept thinking over and over again about the cruel aphorism, "Laugh, and the world laughs with you; cry, and you cry alone." I felt there was not one soul on earth nor power above with the ability or desire to save me.

I mention power above, for at that time God, or His absence, was never far from my thoughts. At times He appeared to me as a cruel, merciless God sitting in His heavenly abode, laughing at the puny manipulations of man. I could not erase from my mind the deeply pessimistic Yiddish expression, *"Mensh tracht uber Got lacht"* ("Man hopes and dreams while God laughs"). At other times I thought—and what a frightening thing this was—*Perhaps there is no God. Perhaps during all these years I had spent reading the Bible, I was really reading fairy tales. Perhaps while delivering countless sermons about God's goodness, justice, and our responsibilities to Him, I had actually been prattling on like an idiot child. Perhaps I had been deceiving my congregation and myself.*

Providentially, we moved to the Chicago area and found the Grove School. Meeting with Virginia Matson, seeing the staff react to these terribly handicapped children, the love they lavished upon these children, Virginia's great kindness, and the depth of her spiritual resources offered the first glimmer of hope for Michael and enabled me to see that people can care, can love, and can believe in spite of great tragedies in their lives.

I also recalled a meeting I had with Isaac a few months before we moved. He was teaching at our alma mater, had married a lovely girl, and they now had one child. He kept in touch with David, who had accepted a position in Canada and was also married. I was still so miserable and ashamed that I could not tell him about Michael. When he asked me about my family I just said that I had two boys.

Isaac invited me to come visit his home and spend a Sunday together with his family. "Sure," I said, "that's a great idea. I'll have Frances call your wife and we'll set the date." I never told Frances and she never called. I was so preoccupied with my own misery that I felt twinges of envy for the happiness Isaac and David had finally found.

Now that I look back, I can begin to comprehend the enormous strength of character my two roommates possessed. How had they managed to survive the concentration camps emotionally intact? How had they broken through the wall of utter despair and total loneliness that must have enveloped them in the nightmarish hell of the Nazi death camps? Even after their liberation, as they took stock of their lives: fathers, mothers, brothers, sisters, friends, all gone, all dead—where had they found the courage, in spite of the horrors of their young lives, to start anew, to marry and bring children into this world?

They had found their strength from the same Source that had enabled millions of Jews for two thousand years to live, dream, and hope in spite of persecution, pogroms, expulsions, and the ultimate horror of Auschwitz. They maintained their faith in God, believing in His ultimate justice and mercy, in His nearness. And this belief had given Isaac and David, like their forefathers, the courage and strength to survive and grow.

The ancient psalmist pondering his own suffering found comfort in the presence of God:

Nevertheless I am continually with Thee;
Thou holdest my right hand.
Thou wilt guide me with Thy counsel,
And afterward receive me with glory.
Whom have I in heaven but Thee?
And beside Thee I desire none upon earth.
My flesh and my heart faileth;
But God is the rock of my heart and my portion for ever.
For, lo, they that go far from Thee shall perish;
Thou dost destroy all them that go astray from Thee.
But as for me, the nearness of God is my good;
I have made the Lord God my refuge,
That I may tell all Thy works.

Psalm 73:23-28

As I now turned to God feeling comforted by His presence the overpowering sense of loneliness began to recede. I was no longer alone.

9
Building Bridges

The great sixteenth-century English poet and clergyman John Donne wrote:

> No man is an island entire of itself, everyman is a piece of the continent, a part of the main, if a clod be washed away by the sea, Europe is the less, as well as if a promontory were, as well as if a manor of thy friends or of thine own were: any man's death diminishes me, because I am involved in mankind; and therefore never send to know for whom the bell tolls, it tolls for thee.

Until we determined that Michael had brain damage, I thought that I was an exception and could live as "an island entire of itself." I considered myself very self-reliant and quite capable of handling my own problems. Even as a child, I had found it hard to ask for help. I can't remember asking my parents for a toy except when I was ill. I did my own homework, never requesting my parents' aid or telephoning a classmate. Although my father was a rabbi, I never wanted him to work with me on my Bible, Hebrew, or Talmud studies. Perhaps this was part of my legacy as an only child, or simply an expression of the great American frontier tradition of independence and self-reliance as expressed in the stories of the wild West and the intrepid, solitary cowboy. However, I think that the main reason I wanted to think I could be independent was the very immature, prideful notion that asking for help was a sign of weakness.

After we found out about Michael's handicap, I couldn't possibly conceive of myself as capable of single-handedly solving my problems. But I was so shocked, ashamed, depressed, and I felt so completely neglected and alone that it made no difference. I still could not turn to anyone for help.

The restoration of my faith in God tore down the wall of isolation, while the Grove School aided me in realizing that there were individuals who wanted to help. I began to attend parents' organization meetings and openly discuss my child's handicap. It was good therapy. As I mentioned earlier, Virginia Matson asked me to conduct a Chanukah assembly for the children, explain the holiday, light the Chanukah candles, and sing appropriate songs. The first year was very difficult for me. A few children were carried into the hall, one of the youngsters let out a shriek every twenty seconds or so, and a boy ran up to me, grabbed a candle, and began eating it. All these children were handicapped. Many of them had multiple handicaps. My heart ached so for these children and the parents that I wanted to cry, but I finished the program, and I have returned to lead a service each year since that first one.

A few months after I moved to Aurora, I was asked to join the board of the local Family Counseling Service, somewhat similar to a mental health clinic. The previous rabbi had served on the board and, in a sense, I was being asked to take his place. I didn't particularly want to; I thought I might be overextending myself during my first year in a new community plus my doctoral studies. In addition, Michael and his future were constantly on my mind.

Yet I agreed to join the board, and I am glad I did. I am now president of Family Counseling. I find my involvement in planning for its future growth exciting and the contact with its director and staff exhilarating. Most of all, I cherish the occasional contact with a client who needs and is getting help. I sat in briefly while an alcoholic who had lost his wife, his job, and his home, was given the address of the local A.A. chapter, an appointment with a prospective employer, and the address of a temporary home. I stood in the waiting room and watched while a teen-ager, pitifully thin and fragile-looking, ran excitedly into the office and proudly announced to her counselor that she had finally succeeded in a task and might be on the road to recovery. My admiration for the people who can offer such help is boundless, and I find a sense of inner satisfaction in the realization that I too am part of this helping process.

The past year I have become involved in working with mentally retarded adults. The state of Illinois has wisely started to move its retarded adults from the larger state-run institutions to much smaller regional centers operated by private concerns where the state pays for the care of the retarded. A year and a half ago, one such regional center was opened in North Aurora in a building previously used as a motel. A few weeks later I received a phone call asking if some people from the Aurora Center could attend Friday evening services. I had never heard of the Aurora Center, but the temple receives many requests from various church groups, schools, and centers who want to attend a Jewish service, and of course I said yes. I think a few congregants were dismayed to find retarded men and women at the services. This was the first time I had encountered the very unpleasant fact about society's reaction to the retarded. There are some people who are bothered by the presence of the retarded, repelled by their appearance. Why? Do these "normal" people think that retardation is contagious? Or do they feel guilty because they are "normal," uncomfortable at the sight of a deformity?

A few days after they first came to services, a member of my congregation called to say, "I just finished talking to someone—I can't tell you her name, but she attends pretty regularly—and she didn't like sitting at services with the retarded." I answered that I was sorry this woman felt the way she did, but as long as I was rabbi, they would be welcome. I am happy to note that we have had no drop in attendance, although the retarded have been coming every week; I have never heard another complaint.

A week before the High Holy Days, I asked the director of the center if I could meet with the Jewish residents before Rosh Hashanah, explain the meaning of these holidays to them on their intellectual level, and tell them what to expect when they attended the High Holy Day services at our temple. I was delighted in their response to the class; they sat quietly listening to everything I said and were so genuinely happy in my coming and teaching them about their faith that I have continued meeting with them every Sunday for an hour. We sing a few Hebrew songs, recite the *Shema* ("Hear, O Israel"), and I tell them Bible stories. Before a Jewish holiday, some of the teen-agers from the temple come with me to help in arranging a party for the center residents, singing songs and playing games with them.

Occasionally I meet one of the retarded person's family, and they invariably express deep gratitude to me for working with their son or daughter, brother or sister. A father once said, "Thank you for doing this . . ." and then his voice trailed off, while his eyes asked the question *But why are you coming? We usually don't expect this from outsiders.*

I answered, "I have a son who is handicapped." We understood each other.

I think of my work with the retarded, or at the Grove School, or as past president of the Parents' Organization for Special Education as part of my answer to the problems of shame, the sense of helplessness in the face of tragedy. I had first to find God and then my fellow sufferer. I want to try and build a bridge between myself and those who share my sorrow, because they too have afflicted children. I see no difference in color between us, or religion, or education, or income.

The most personal and most important prayer on Yom Kippur is the confession of sin that concludes the *Amidah*, the silent devotion. I stand away from my neighbor, so that he cannot overhear me and I can confess in solitude. I feel as if I were the only person in the sanctuary, a single human being in communion with God. Yet I say these prayers in the plural: "For the sin which we have committed before Thee under compulsion or of our own will, and for the sin which we have committed before Thee by hardening our hearts . . . ." I continue in this manner reciting a number of paragraphs, enumerating various sins, and always in the plural. Judaism reminds me, in this most sacred of all days, that I am part of a community and a nation, that I am responsible not only for my actions but also for my neighbor's deeds, and that I may turn to him for solace and strength. "Am I my brother's keeper?" the murderer Cain asked God. If I am to remain human, if I am to be comforted, then I must answer yes. I must keep on building bridges.

10
Love and Courage

I vividly remember how Frances looked when she walked into the dining room of a Catskill Mountain resort and into my life. She is five feet tall, and standing next to her girlfriend who was five feet six inches, she looked even smaller. She had not slept for twenty-four hours; this was the first time she had ever been away from Chicago; and appearing younger than her nineteen years, she seemed like a lost, shy, forlorn young girl.

She insists that the moment she saw me she fell in love. I can't say the same, but I did know that she was someone special. We sat at the same dining room table, walked in the woods together, swam, went boating, and played volleyball together. I should have proposed that week to this small, beautiful girl who was (after a little sleep) bursting with youth and life, laughter and love. Instead we dated the two months she stayed in New York City before returning to Chicago. After she left I realized how much I loved and missed her and how empty my life had become without her. She came back to New York in October, and the following year we were married.

The first few years of marriage were marvelously happy ones. We were very much in love, slowly discovering the depths of our feelings. When Adam first saw Eve in the Garden of Eden he said, "This is now bone of my bones, and flesh of my flesh." I felt that Frances was part of me, that we were now one. How could I have lived for twenty-six years without her? The world was so beautiful because of her. And then we had Michael. Our joy was complete. The diagnosis of Michael's handicap irrevocably changed the situation. For a week I didn't even tell my parents, but sooner or later they had to be told, and it had best be sooner. I knew what a terrible shock the news would be. Michael was their first grandchild and had been given the name of my mother's father, a saintly scribe who had died a few years before in the Holy Land. When I told my mother the news, my father was out completing last-minute details for their forthcoming move to Israel. She didn't cry. She sat, her eyes looking into the distance as if in prayer, and after a while said, "I want you to promise me one thing. I want you to promise that you and Frances will have more children." *What's the use of arguing?* I thought, but having more children was the furthest thing from my mind. We sat talking softly for another half-hour. My mother wanted to postpone their move. She was certain Frances would need help with the children. Michael was at his most hyperactive, and Steve was little more than a year old. How could she leave us at this particular time? I insisted that they go. They had dreamed of Israel for a lifetime. Why add to a tragic situation by shattering my parents' dream as ours had been destroyed? Finally I left. The subject of the promise had not been broached again.

When we were first married, Frances and I had talked about having a fairly large family. As an only child, I wanted my children to avoid that experience. Frances has a younger brother with whom we are close, but she had also been unsatisfied and had envied those of her friends with a number of brothers and sisters. "We'll have at least two boys and two girls," I said, "so I can play ball with the boys while Frances dresses the girls in beautiful clothing and has long girl-to-girl talks with them when they become teen-agers." We joked about the biblical command "Be fruitful and multiply," which was the first commandment given to Adam and Eve in the Garden of Eden. At least we would try to fulfill this *mitzvah* even if we failed to uphold any other.

But how could we now consider having another child? Thank God, Steve was born before we even suspected that Michael wasn't normal. Now that we knew, to plan for another child was unthinkable. We couldn't imagine our life returning to a semblance of normalcy, much less facing the prospect of another baby.

During the next few months Frances displayed more loving care and courage than I could ever match. I did not have the fortitude to take Michael to the various doctors. She did. I could not sit with Michael in the waiting rooms of hospitals, calm his fears, persuade him to allow the nurses to take blood for countless tests and hear the seemingly hopeless prognosis of the experts. She could. I would flee from Michael's presence, his tantrums, his wildness; I would go to my office in the temple, close the door, and try unsuccessfully to erase the cries from my mind while Frances stayed with Michael.

Yet his affliction never became the overriding concern and passion of her life. Many marriages have collapsed under the pressure of a handicapped child, with the mother devoting herself completely to the youngster and neglecting the rest of the family, or the father failing to cope with the tragedy and running away, spiritually if not physically. At night we would fall asleep tightly holding each other, finding warmth and comfort in our deepening love.

I cannot recall that year without giving thanks to the Lord for the one life-giving force that sustained me—our love for each other. Had it not been for our love, I don't believe that I could have survived either spiritually or emotionally. I had lost faith in God and myself. My world had come to an end. Only my belief in our love enabled me to endure.

Two, three years passed. We were now living in Aurora and had found the Grove School. Michael was making progress and we could hope that he might yet develop into some sort of a person.

"Hy, I think that it's about time we had another child," Frances suddenly said one evening after we attended a meeting of the Grove School parents organization.

"How are you going to take care of Michael, drive him daily to school while you're pregnant or the baby is an infant?"

"We'll plan to have her" (Frances was sure the baby would be a girl) "in the late spring so you won't have to drive very long. And when the fall term starts, she'll be old enough to take along."

"What if the baby isn't normal? I know this can happen in any family, but it's already happened to us. Suppose we have another Michael or worse?"

No doctor could explain to us how Michael had become brain-damaged. We were certain that it had not happened after birth. He had had no illness that might have triggered the damage. We didn't know of any retarded child in our immediate family, and the delivery had been normal, but no doctor could reassure us that this would not happen again. Lightning, in the case of an abnormal baby, can and frequently does strike more than once.

Finally I agreed with her. We would dare to have another child. How we prayed that this was the right decision.

I had always thought of courage as synonymous with valor and bravery, a soldier charging the enemy lines or a saint walking to his death with a prayer on his lips rather than forsaking his faith. Part of the service during Yom Kippur is dedicated to the memory of ten sages and martyrs who were tortured by their Roman captors in an attempt to break their will. I cried as I read the account of Rabbi Akiva's death, the inner strength that enabled him to say at the very moment his flesh was being torn off: "Happy am I that I have finally been afforded the opportunity to fulfill God's commandment, 'Thou shalt love the Lord thy God with all thy heart, with all thy soul, and with all thy might,' for now I may give my very soul to the Lord."

Courage for me was associated with great acts of heroism in the face of death. I learned from Frances that a reaffirmation of life in the face of tragedy can require as much if not more courage.

I cannot overemphasize her courage in saying, "Yes, we must have another child." Every mother goes through the nine months of pregnancy with mixed emotions of joy and fear—joy in feeling the life in her womb, fear that something may be wrong with the infant growing within her. How much greater was to be my wife's fear. I could offer her some comfort by giving her as much love and affection as possible. But in the middle of the night, as she lay awake feeling the movement of our unborn child, beset by terrible anxieties of the unknown future, only her indomitable courage buttressed by the growing faith that God would watch over us, calmed her and offered her the peace of mind that saw her through those anxiety-filled months.

On Monday afternoon, June 6, 1966, she gave birth to a seven-pound two-ounce baby girl. We named her Alexandra in memory of my father. In retrospect, the name took on a deeper symbolic meaning to us. The Hebrew definition of *Alexandra* is "God is salvation."

Our fears concerning the newborn baby, however, were not yet over. Alexandra's feet turned in, and our pediatrician advised us to see an orthopedic doctor immediately since she might have a club foot. How frightening these words were to us. Had our prayers gone unheeded? Had God forsaken us? Fortunately, the orthopedic doctor reassured us that Alexandra did not have a club foot. He said he would begin correcting her turned-in feet by putting them in casts immediately; x-rays were taken of both hips. These x-rays showed that the hip bone was not growing properly into the socket, but this too was corrected with a special harness which she wore for a year. Had Alexandra's feet not turned in, we would have never x-rayed her hips, and had we not discovered this at so early an age when it was easily correctible, she could have dislocated her hip when she began to walk and been crippled for life. God had been merciful to us.

During Alexandra's first few months, I would tiptoe into her room almost nightly to see if she were still alive. Frances had recurrent nightmares in which she saw the baby suffocating or crippled. We've kept baby record books recording Michael and Steve's development. When Alexandra was seven months old, we began to worry because she hadn't started to stand. Steve stood at seven months, although he also wore a crossbar for turned-in feet. She stood two weeks later. Then every night when I came home I would ask Frances, "Has the baby started walking yet?" She began to walk a month after Steve.

Today she is a normal, lovely, talkative eight-year-old, perhaps a bit spoiled, but a joy to the whole family.

Frances taught me so much about courage. The courageous person is not necessarily one who feels no fear; in fact, courage and fear frequently go hand in hand. We were terribly afraid before we decided to have another baby. We were afraid all during those nine long months. We were even afraid during the first few years of Alexandra's life, during the time her feet were being corrected, before she took her first steps, before she spoke her first words, before she said her first sentence. We were afraid that perhaps she would not walk at all, perhaps she would not talk. We are probably more concerned about the health and well-being of our children than parents who have not had a handicapped child, but we were able to overcome these fears. The true mark of courage is to recognize one's fear and to do what is right in spite of it.

I learned that it can take as much courage to live as to die, and that it may call for even more courage to reaffirm life by bringing a new life into this world. I recall reading a most beautiful interpretation of the meaning behind the biblical book of Job written by the noted Jewish author Eli Weisel. He noted that the ultimate answer given to those who ask, "Why do the righteous suffer?" is found not in God's words out of the whirlwind but in the epilogue itself.

So the Lord blessed the latter end of Job more than his beginning; and he had fourteen thousand sheep, and six thousand camels, and a thousand yoke of oxen, and a thousand she-asses. He had also seven sons and three daughters. And he called the name of the first, Jemimah; and the name of the second, Keziah; and the name of the third, Keren-happuch. And in all the land were no women found so fair as the daughters of Job; and their father gave them inheritance among their brethren. And after this Job lived a hundred and forty years, and saw his sons, and his sons' sons, even four generations. So Job died, being old and full of days.

Job 42:12-17

After all Job's suffering, after the destruction of his property, the death of his children, his own horrible afflictions, and the terrible doubts he had—Job found the courage to start life anew, to rebuild his home, to remake his fortune, and once again to bring children into the world.

Eli Weisel noted that he had found the same courageous attitude among the survivors of Hitler's infamous death camps. They too had returned from hell, a hell created by man himself on this earth, yet they were prepared not only to continue living but also to marry and give birth to children. Mr. Weisel should know the meaning of courage, for as a teen-ager he lived through Auschwitz and has had the strength to write about these experiences so that the world would know the story of this infamous camp.

Jewish history is replete with sagas of tragedy, persecution, and death. Yet through it all, the Jew has retained his faith in God, and Judaism has maintained an optimistic view of the future, a belief in a world where "Nation shall not lift up sword against nation, neither shall men learn war anymore." Two thousand years after the destruction of the Temple in Jerusalem and the dispersion of the Jewish people to the four corners of the earth, a segment has had the courage to rebuild the land of Israel, the home of their forefathers, despite the dangers they face and the perils of this new beginning.

Love and Courage

Suffering is part of life. It is the crux of Job's dilemma, the burden of the Jewish people, and in a real sense, the cross we must all bear. At times I was sorely tempted to rail against my burden, to give up hope and call quits on life. I had even lost faith in God. But as my faith slowly began to return, my attitude towards the tragedies inherent in life changed. If I stood upright, put my ultimate fate into God's hands, and started rebuilding, I could make a life that would be full of joy and love. It calls for a courage that says *yes* to life, that says, *Recognize your fears and learn to live with them,* that says, *God is good; God is kind; trust Him, and He will reward you.*

While talking to parents of the retarded at the Aurora Center, the conversation often gets around to other members of the family. "Does Jimmy have a brother or sister? " I ask. "No, he's the only one. After him, well, we just couldn't have another." I feel so sorry for these people. They have devoted all their life to this handicapped son or daughter.

God was so good to us (though at the time we would never have thought it) in hiding Michael's affliction from us until Steve was born. Would we have had another child if Steve had not been alive when the pediatrician said, "Michael has brain damage"? Even so, the joy we have experienced through our children could never have taken place without the love and courage of my beautiful Frances.

97

11
A Unique Child

But what of Michael? What is he like? How has he reacted to all that has happened to him?

He was born at four o'clock in the morning on October 6, 1959, in New Grace Hospital, Detroit. It was a day after Rosh Hashanah, and Frances had spent the holiday at temple, afraid she would have to go to the hospital while I was conducting services. Michael held out. When I returned from a congregational meeting, Frances greeted me with the news: "I think I'm having labor pains."

It rained that night, and I recall thinking, *It rained the night the heroine in Hemingway's* Farewell to Arms *was having a baby, and she died.* We drove to the hospital. I had settled Frances in her room when the nurse came in and said, "You can go home and get some sleep. She won't be due for hours." Ten minutes after I had walked back into our apartment, the phone rang. "Mr. Agress, please come back to the hospital; your wife was just wheeled into the delivery room." As I stepped into the hospital lobby, the obstetrician greeted me with *"Mazel tov*—it's a 6½-pound boy, and he and mother are doing well. You'll be able to see her in another hour."

I attended early morning services at my temple even though I had had no sleep. I wanted to thank God properly.

A Unique Child

Did the injury to Michael's brain occur during delivery? At the time the doctor told me that it had been a quick and uncomplicated birth. We've tortured ourselves trying to think of any accident during Michael's first year, but we've found nothing. Frances had no complications during pregnancy, took no harmful medicines or drugs. Ultimately science may find that there was an undetected defect in our genes that could cause this type of disability in an unborn infant. Perhaps the anesthesia administered during delivery cut off the necessary oxygen to the unborn baby's brain. We shall never be certain, but whatever the cause, the damage was done.

Now, as I think back, I can recall a number of times during the first year and a half when I worried about Michael's development, but I always pushed it aside with the thought, *There can't be anything wrong with him. Spock says that each child develops differently. It couldn't happen to me.* The first summer we brought him to New York my mother asked, "Why doesn't he sit up by himself? He's eight months old." "You're just a typical Jewish grandmother worried about every little thing," we replied. "He's a fat baby and too top-heavy. You've always been a nervous person, but we won't raise our children that way." At the end of the summer he did sit by himself.

Michael didn't start walking until quite late. Frances had gone into the hospital to have Steve by induced labor. Both grandparents were staying at our apartment in Detroit to help the expectant mother. Michael had a bloody nose which was hard to stop, and the two worried grandmothers took him to our pediatrician. Frances was still not in the labor room, and I returned home to learn what the doctor had said about Michael.

"It's nothing serious, just some weak blood vessels," one of the grandmothers noted, "but the doctor wants to take some tests of Michael's brain."

"If there isn't anything wrong with his nose, why the brain tests?"

I was panicky; Frances was in the hospital having a baby, perhaps at this moment, and something might be wrong with Michael's brain. I called the doctor immediately. "I wouldn't be worried, rabbi," he said, "but you know the way grandmothers are. To relieve their worry, I told them that we would take an electroencephalogram of Michael's brain if he hasn't started walking in two weeks." I returned to the hospital somewhat calmed—to find Frances in hard labor. I called the nurse, who promptly wheeled her in the delivery room. A half-hour later she gave birth to a six-pound six-ounce baby boy we called Stephen Joseph.

For the next two weeks, I kept walking Michael, having him hold my fingers, urging him to take a step by himself until finally he did. I could relax. I didn't have to worry or bring him in for an EEG. I later learned from a leading pediatric neurologist that infant EEGs rarely prove anything.

One summer before Michael's handicap was diagnosed we spent a day with a dear friend of ours. During the visit she told us some news about a little girl we all knew who had lived in the apartment next to ours. She was a wild child, destructive, running about day and night, always climbing trees, never able to sit quietly in class for more than a few minutes. I would now call her hyperactive. At that time I had never heard the word. Her parents had taken her to a neurologist, and he found that something was physically wrong with her. She was now in a hospital.

I couldn't sleep that night. I finally woke Frances. "I'm worried about Michael," I said. "Maybe he's also sick. He sounds like Trudy, the little girl in Detroit."

"I really don't think so," she answered, "and anyhow, Michael has his yearly appointment with the pediatrician a month from now." Later Frances told me that she was also worried, but she wanted to calm me and so she lied. The month flew by, Michael's appointment came, and we heard the word *brain-damaged.*

It is an all-inclusive word and a poor description of the malady. Some children have a brain dysfunction, and after a number of years the brain may mature sufficiently so that after the teen years they may function normally, while in other instances, there has been actual damage to a part of the brain. Some brain-damaged children may have normal or above-normal intelligence. Many experts in the field now believe that as many as five to ten percent of the children in our public schools suffer from some form of minimal brain-damage dysfunction or perceptual handicaps. Youngsters who at one time were called lazy readers, nervous, high-strung, or antisocial, have been found to suffer from some sort of physiological disability. Other brain-damaged children are intellectually slow or retarded, while some youngsters with more than minimal brain damage may be so perceptually handicapped that normal intelligence testing is almost useless. Michael is in this classification. He has tested retarded, but his teachers feel that these tests cannot factually determine his true capabilities.

Recently I took Michael to an optometrist who specializes in testing the vision of these types of problem children. I sat in on the examination, and it was a revelation to me. Michael always had great difficulties in doing picture puzzles. At the age of six he could not do the puzzles of a 2½-year-old. I had assumed that this was due to retardation. During the eye examination, we found that Michael cannot distinguish, with any degree of accuracy, shapes and figures. Either because of an eye malfunction, or else because the message his eye sends to his brain is scrambled, he does not see shapes properly. He cannot catch a ball. I had thought he was lazy or just slow. The doctor showed me that he did not see the thrown ball. He located it only by listening to it pass him and fall to the ground. Yet he is not blind. In fact, he has normal vision as vision is usually tested, but he is visually handicapped.

How frightening this world must seem to Michael. How disturbing everything must be. He sees what we do not see, and fails to see what we see. The most fearful aspect of all must be the demands we made upon him, to which he could never respond physically. How destructive this must have been to his self-confidence, to his appreciation of his own abilities. And vision is but part of his disability. He hears us, but what he hears may be distorted. Once again, as with his vision, his hearing per se is normal, but it may become scrambled on the way to the brain. Michael's teacher recently cited an example of just such a problem that was almost funny. The class had been reading, and at the conclusion of the lesson, the teacher told them to put their books on their desks. Michael took all his books from his cupboard and put them on his desk. (At this point, it reminded me of an old Marx Brothers comedy routine. Much of their comedy was based on the quite literal interpretation of a statement. Michael had done exactly that.) He had taken his teacher's instruction literally. Yet we know that he comprehends what he reads and he reads at his own age level.

Michael is hyperactive. Maturity has quieted him down to a certain extent and he has also been taking medication in the morning and when he goes to sleep, but he still cannot concentrate for any length of time. His is easily distracted. His motor activity is very poor.

He is emotionally immature. As a baby he could not relate to us as a normal infant. For the first few months of his life, he had a crying period of an hour to an hour and a half every night. When he came home from the hospital he had his nights and days mixed up. Our pediatrician prescribed phenobarbital so that he could straighten himself out internally. Yet though we took him into our arms and into our bed and cuddled him, we were never able to stop his crying. Only walking or rocking seemed to help. When, as a baby, either Steve or Alexandra fell or hurt themselves, we calmed them by holding and kissing them. It never worked with Michael. He resisted every attempt on our part to soothe him. We were even unable to hold and play with him. He detested this; he hated almost any feeling of constriction. He didn't let us put a bandage on him. As he grew into a toddler, we had to hold him down physically for the doctor to examine him. Much if not all of this is due to his brain dysfunction and consequent hyperactivity, but at the time we didn't know it and were completely baffled by his behavior. The brain is the most complicated instrument imaginable. We haven't come within miles of duplicating, with our most sophisticated computers, God's creation—the human mind, the brain, and the nervous system. Our brain receives millions of daily impressions and instructions that are either filed away or acted upon. What happens when something goes haywire in this intricate mechanism? This, to a greater or lesser degree, happens to all brain-damaged children. How difficult it must be for these children to cope with our world. How terrifying it can become for them.

Cataloging all of Michael's disabilities may give a sense of the enormous dimensions of his problems. It does not begin to explain his character, the unique facets of his personality. For the longest time I did not even begin to fathom the depth of my son's inner resources. I was so wholly preoccupied with my own grief, concerned with the personal woes and the emotional and religious upheaval taking place within me, that I could not see him tentatively groping toward a form of self-expression that might give him both self-respect and a life of his own. That he was able to do this, in spite of all his handicaps, is a tribute to his own great courage, persistence, and innate capabilities. It is a mark of the individuality that exists in all of God's creations.

It is hard for me to convey the sense of frustration we felt in attempting to cope with his hyperactivity. Nothing helped. We tried to interest him in the various toys children play with. He would try one toy, then another, then a third, discarding each after a few minutes and running from place to place. When my wife took him shopping, he darted from aisle to aisle touching everything, interested in nothing. The only way that we could control him was quite literally by forcibly holding him down. We did find, however, that certain music could soothe him.

Interestingly enough it had to be classical or semiclassical music.

Finally, almost in sheer desperation, my wife began to take out children's books from the public library and read to Michael. We hoped that reading to him would quiet him down, at least temporarily, and that it might even help his speech. At that time, he didn't say a word. Even this didn't help. He listened for a moment and then turned away, or he began to flip pages in a haphazard and seemingly uncontrollable fashion.

After a while we noticed an interesting thing happening. Michael stopped at a particular word and pointed to it. My wife repeated the word. He would stare at the word for an instant, and then continue turning the pages, while Frances desperately tried to interest him in the story itself. On the next day or week, when she returned to the same story, Michael would once again point to that particular word, Frances would repeat it out loud, Michael would stare and then continue the same process of turning pages. After a while, he would pick up the book himself, flip the pages, find the particular word, and bring it to us. We found, in fact, that he would point to that same word in other books.

One of Michael's favorite words was *stop*. He pointed to it every time he noticed it in a book. As we walked together down the street, he would run to the stop sign. In a great state of excitement he would seem to be begging us to repeat the word. It is the one word that remains fixed in my mind, although I paid very little attention to it then. Now, after seeing his development, I wonder whether he was not expressing a deep psychologically felt need in singling out that particular word. Perhaps he was attempting to tell himself: *I must* stop *this wildness, I must* stop *this random activity.* As I learn more and more about him and his truly dramatic, deep insights, I begin to think that he may well have understood what he was doing when he pointed to that particular word.

When we began taking Michael to the nursery school which was part of the Albert Einstein Medical Center in New York, we told the nursery school supervisor of Michael's reading habits and that we thought he was trying to learn how to read. Since he did not talk, we could not be certain, but intuitively we felt this was what he was trying to do. She discouraged us. "Children of Michael's age aren't supposed to read. Get him to play with toys and do things more suitable for his age." We followed her instructions and told him it wasn't important for him to read. Thank the good Lord, he didn't listen to us and continued to identify more and more words.

I should not be too critical of the teacher; it was she who first proved to us that Michael was far more perceptive than we had ever imagined. She showed us that there were times when he was making fools of us. We would talk to him, order him to do something, and get not even a flicker of response. We knew he could hear. Since he was brain-damaged, we thought he was so retarded he didn't understand. She ordered us to "Be firm with Michael when you want him to do something. Tell him in no uncertain terms that he must do such and such a thing, and if he does not listen, he will be punished."

Her advice worked. Frances would order Michael to pick up a book. No response. She would then add, "Michael, if you don't pick up the book, I am going to shut off the record player and you won't be allowed to listen to the music." Immediately he picked up the book. He was doing what most children do—tune out their mothers and fathers. Had the teacher not brought this to our attention, we would not have realized that Michael was capable of acting in this manner.

The same thing was happening to Michael's toilet training. He was four years old when we brought him to the nursery, and he hadn't started to become toilet-trained. She told us to begin immediately by removing his diapers, putting on training pants, and taking him into the bathroom with me when I went. For two weeks we followed her instructions without any results. Michael soiled himself and said nothing. He went into the bathroom with me and showed no interest at all. One Friday evening as I was leaving for services at temple, I told

Michael I wanted him to go to the bathroom by himself. I returned home to find Frances excited and all smiles. A half-hour after I had left, Michael, without saying a word to her, had gone into the bathroom, pulled down his training pants, urinated, pulled up his pants, and walked out. It seemed to us nearly miraculous. In fact, it was only the first of many occasions when we felt a sense of wonderment about Michael, a feeling almost of a miracle occuring.

Michael went to the nursery school for one year. He was still hyperactive. He did not talk. He did not play with toys or other children, but there were changes in him that enabled us to hope for a better future. He was toilet-trained. Above all, we began to realize that he had much more within him than we had ever imagined.

The following year we moved to Aurora and began to look for a suitable school. As months passed and we still could find no school or help for Michael, his intellectual and emotional growth seemed to stop, even retrogress. No doubt our frustrations and feeling of hopelessness had an effect upon him, for he has always been sensitive to the smallest emotional upset. Yet during all this time he continued opening books and pointing to certain words. He was slowly and diligently going about this particular task of his.

Finally we found the Grove School. He began to attend classes, and shortly after that, he started to use words. He could not speak sentences, but he had finally begun to express himself verbally. I thanked God!

The highly technical, urbanized civilization we live in does not extoll a child like Michael. It is an age of huge machines, sophisticated computers, masses of people. According to various scientists we are in danger of destroying ourselves by overpopulation. We think of man as a small, expendable cog in this vast apparatus we call modern society. Whenever I fall into this type of reverie and sense the danger of self-deprecation and denial of my humanity, I try to think of Michael. He is handicapped, yet so unique. Michael is for me a symbol of the

A Unique Child

miraculous in God's creations, the individuality of His concern.

The ancient Jewish sages, while discussing the philosophical question of why man was initially created as a single being on earth, give the following moral interpretation:

> See how many animals there are in the world, and how many beasts there are in the world, and how many fish there are in the world; is the voice of any one of them like any other? Or the appearance of any one of them like the appearance of any other? Or the sense of any one of them like the sense of any other? Or the taste of any one of them like the taste of any other? Why, neither in voice, nor in appearance, nor in sense, nor in taste are they alike?

The masters have taught:

> This is to tell you the greatness of the King who is King over all kings, the Holy One, blessed be He; for a man stamps many coins in one mold and they are all alike; but the King who is King over all kings, the Holy One, blessed be He, stamped every man in the mold of the first man, yet not one of them resembles his fellow. Hence it is said: "How great are Thy works, O Lord."

These ancient sages speak to all men. It is a personal message to me, for Michael is my son and he has helped to show me God's wonder.

I thank the Lord every day that Michael was born in this generation and not thirty years sooner. Had he been born then, when no one had an appreciation of brain damage, perceptual handicaps, and the complexities of the problem, he would have been diagnosed as hopelessly retarded. As his parents, we would have been urged to put him away in an institution. I thank God Michael is part of our family and has such unique attributes. He exemplifies the miraculous manifested in all of God's creations.

12
The Real Michael

Michael has exceedingly grave problems, and there is no minimizing the great difficulties he faces. Because of his perceptual disabilities, he sees an alien and disturbing world. His hyperactivity doesn't allow him to sit still or concentrate on one specific project. It robs him of the self-satisfaction a normal child has in accomplishing a task. He feels timid, uncertain of himself. In the past, he would automatically say "I don't know" to any question we asked, or "Help me" to any job we gave him, although we knew that he could answer the question or do the job. "I don't know" and "help me" were expressions of his deep sense of inadequacy. It is a mark of the distance Michael has come in the past few years to note the decrease in his use of those phrases.

One can imagine the emotional and physical strain that this placed on Frances and myself. For the longest time we were simply overwhelmed by him and his problems. We felt completely lost, almost as helpless as Michael.

Yet there were moments in those dark days when it seemed as if by divine providence we could detect another Michael, a different person, a gentle being, a courageous child with a mind and a heart and a soul that were uniquely his. Those moments stood out in such contrast to the handicapped and all but useless child he appeared to be. Only now have we learned to esteem other facets of his wonderful nature.

I can recall, as if it were yesterday, the first time we noticed Michael's love of music. We had just learned of his brain damage. Our pediatrician had prescribed pills to quiet him; this, however, had produced the opposite effect. Not only was he hyperactive, but, under the influence of the medication, he had become despondent and ultrasensitive. He was constantly crying and banging his head against the wall. One evening, in an attempt to distract myself and quiet the turmoil whirling in my mind, I turned on the television and started watching Leonard Bernstein conduct the New York Philharmonic. Michael heard me switch on the set and ran into the room. As soon as he heard the music and saw the orchestra, he plumped himself down on the couch and sat transfixed for an hour through the whole concert. Neither Frances nor I had ever seen him sit so still for such a length of time. The music proved to have "charms to soothe the savage beast."

This was the beginning of an ongoing love affair between Michael and music. He finds in it an emotional outlet. He has an ear for music. He can remember tunes much more readily than either Frances or I or either of our other children. As wild as he was, he could always be calmed by a gentle and melodious tune. On the other hand, discordant or off-key notes will drive him to distraction.

We were always concerned when we took him visiting to another house. He did not sit still or play with toys. Yet he always approached a piano with reverential care. Instead of banging on the keyboard, he gently pushed down the keys with one or two fingers. The first time he did this, we were astonished. We were visiting relatives and were sitting in another room when we suddenly heard someone picking away at the piano in an attempt to find a tune. When we walked into the room, we were amazed to find him sitting at the piano with a music score in front of him. Four-year-old Michael was trying to play the piano and at the same time read the musical score.

Music has done more than soothe Michael or offer him certain aesthetic satisfactions. He has used it to help him learn how to read. He has used it to open up new worlds for himself.

We recently purchased a stereo record player. I had hoped to sit back on an evening in my favorite easy chair and relax while listening to fine music. I haven't had much time for that sort of leisure, but Michael uses it constantly. When he comes home from school, he asks Frances to turn on the stereo and play his favorite records while he lies on the carpet and listens. Among his favorite pieces is an album of Gilbert and Sullivan music, including the "Mikado," "H.M.S. Pinafore," and others of their classic songs. Included in this album is a booklet with the libretto of both shows and the songs. When he plays these records, he opens the booklet and follows along with the songs just like a music lover listening to his favorite opera with the libretto open in his lap. If Michael thinks no one is watching, he will even sing along and wave his arms in imitation of a musical conductor, lifting his hands when the music reaches a crescendo, lowering them when a passage concludes.

Recently he has taught himself how to play music. We have an old children's xylophone, and every so often he goes down to the children's playroom and removes the xylophone from the shelf. Softly striking it with his small wooden hammer, he picks out a tune. He knows when he has struck a wrong or discordant note; when this happens, he starts over again until he finally hits the right key.

My brother-in-law and his wife have an old piano in their Chicago apartment. When we visit them, all our children rush to the piano and try to play it. Alexandra pounds away; Steve tries to pick out a tune but quickly becomes discouraged. Michael patiently sits at the piano and plays, repeating the tune over and over again until he gets it right.

All this would not be remarkable in a normal child. Many youngsters have taught themselves to play on a piano or a xylophone. However, Michael is not a normal child. He has never shown an ability to stick to a job until satisfactorily com-

110

pleting it. It's much easier for him to give up and ask for help, or say, "I can't do it," but he has never done this with a musical instrument. In fact, he doesn't want to be helped. He wants to play all by himself.

How has this happened? His innate love of music and sense of pitch has helped. But I think most important of all has been our appreciation of this talent and the lack of pressure. When it comes to music, he can do something even his brother cannot duplicate. He need not worry about failure, for he is not asked to succeed. Recently he took part in a school assembly, where he was part of the band and played a cymbal. After the concert I asked the teacher if she knew that he could also play the piano. "Michael," she said, turning to him, "you never told me you could play the piano. Come here and sit down. Let me hear you play something." He sat down at the piano, picked away for a moment in a desultory manner and then just sat and stared. He wasn't about to play for her. At that moment playing had become a pressurized chore, and he wasn't going to respond.

Of particular satisfaction to me was watching and helping Michael acquire a religious education with the aid of music, records, and his remarkable self-taught ability to read. I had always been troubled by the fact that I could not give him the type of religious instruction that my other two children would receive. There is a specialized Jewish parochial school for retarded and brain-damaged children, and there are also Sunday and supplementary weekday classes for these types of youngsters. Unfortunately, they are found only in New York City, on the East Coast, or on Chicago's North Side and the North Shore. This type of formal instruction for Michael was out of the question. Happily, though, Judaism is rich in its various religious holidays, and a good part of the celebration of these holidays occurs in the home.

The classic example of the Jewish home festival is Passover. The major ritual of this holiday is the *Seder* on the first two nights of the festival comprising the Passover meal and a ser-

111

vice preceding it. Traditionally, the children play an important role in the service. They start the *Seder* by chanting the Four Questions beginning with, "Why is this night different from all other nights in the year?" The heart of the service consists of the father's reply to the children, the story of the exodus of the Israelites from Egypt and the Psalms glorifying their miraculous deliverance. When the children were quite young, I purchased a Passover record with some of the popular Passover songs and the Four Questions in Hebrew. I had hoped that the children would enjoy listening to the record and learn something of the service from it. Michael was five at the time, Steve was 3½, and Alexandra had not yet been born.

On this particular Passover, Frances, her parents, the children, and I gathered at our home to celebrate the holiday. I turned to Michael, the eldest son, and asked him if he wanted to sing the Four Questions in Hebrew along with me. Naturally he shook his head no, but we finally coaxed him into trying. We started singing together, and then I stopped while he continued. In a shy, hesitant, yet sweet voice, he finished all by himself, singing the Four Questions. There were tears in our eyes and a beautiful smile on Michael's face.

This particular *Seder* proved but the beginning of Michael's religious experiences.

On Friday evening, the start of our Sabbath, we gather around the table and prepare to eat our meal by singing a special Hebrew prayer which is called the *Kiddush,* the sanctification of the Sabbath over a cup of wine. As my children grew older, I tried to encourage them to sing it along with me. I turned to Steve and asked him if he wanted to chant it by himself. "All right, dad," he replied, "as long as you help me." He sang the *Kiddush* with a good deal of prompting from me. I then turned and said, "Michael, do you want to try?" "No." "I'll help you." Once again, "No." Finally I said, "If you try I'll give you a reward." This offer was too tempting for him to refuse. Not only was he able to chant the Hebrew words of the *Kiddush* prayer, but he was better at it than Steve. He has continued to sing the *Kiddush* every Friday evening and he loves it.

We had, to a certain extent, a similar experience with Michael for the holiday of Chanukah, the festival of light. Chanukah occurs in the wintertime. The reason for the celebration is found in the book of Maccabees. It commemorates the war of independence waged by the ancient state of Israel, led by Judah Maccabee, against their Syrian overlords. The Jewish people have celebrated this festival ever since by lighting candles for eight evenings, chanting blessings, and singing special songs, all in Hebrew. At our home, each child has his or her own small candelabra and repeats the service with me.

I thought I would try the same thing with the Chanukah blessings as I had done with Passover, so I bought a record with both the blessings and the story of the holiday on it. I didn't have to urge Michael to play the record. Every day, as soon as he came home from school, he took off his coat, ran down to his playroom, turned on his children's record player, and put on the Chanukah record. We have four Chanukah menorahs at home; the largest and most elaborate one I light, and the other three are lit by the three youngsters. On the first night of Chanukah I put the candle in the menorah, lit the *shamos* (servant candle), sang the blessings, and kindled the one candle that represents the first night of the holiday. Then I turned to Michael, as the oldest child, and asked, "Michael, do you want to light your menorah and sing the blessing?" I got the expected response: "No." "Come on, Mike, you can do it," Steve and I urged. Finally he assented and sang it softly and accurately.

During that week, I also went to the Grove School to conduct a Chanukah service in front of all the youngsters. I told Michael what I would be doing and that I hoped he would also participate. He dislikes my coming and had on occasion burst out in tears when he saw me in school, but on this occasion he said yes. He didn't like getting up in front of an audience, and even I could barely hear him, but he sang the blessings.

Three months after the Chanukah program, in early spring, we decided to take him to Friday evening services at our temple. On previous occasions, when Frances wanted to attend services either on the High Holy Days or on Friday evening, we got a baby-sitter for Michael, even when we took Steve along. We assumed that he couldn't possibly behave during services. He was much too hyperactive. He couldn't sit for more than a few minutes. We had taken him to a movie during Christmas vacation and it was a nightmarish experience. He constantly squirmed in his seat, continually kicked the seat in front of him, yelled whenever the spirit moved him, and kept running to the lobby for more candy and pop.

Could we expect him to behave any better at temple during a service he could not understand? At least in a movie children were expected to make some noise and we were just part of an anonymous audience, but I was the rabbi at the temple, and one expects certain decorum and quiet during prayers.

Yet we owed it to Michael and ourselves at least to try. I had started going to my father's synagogue at a very early age, and Steve was only three when he first went with us to services. Now that Michael had participated in a Chanukah program at the Grove School and learned both the Four Questions for Passover and the blessings for the candle lighting on Chanukah, he might be ready for attendance at the temple.

After the Sabbath meal, an hour before we were to leave for temple, I called him into the living room for a talk.

"Mike, you're going with us to services tonight. We want you to behave there, not talk or yell or run out of the sanctuary during the whole hour's service. We're going to sing songs in Hebrew and read some prayers. You can try to follow along with mom. I'm going to speak for about twenty minutes, and you must be quiet during that time even if you don't understand what I'm saying. Big boys go to services, and we're taking you because we know that you are a big boy. If you don't behave, mom is going to pull you out of the sanctuary and you will have to sit in my office. If you do behave, we'll reward you with an extra cupcake." He loves to eat, and food, especially cake or raisins, has always been a marvelous form of bribery.

It was nerve-racking hour. He fidgeted, called out occasionally, and Frances had to threaten to pull him out of the sanctuary. But as I looked at him eagerly trying to follow the services, so interested in everything that was happening, his face radiant with a joy that I had rarely seen, I wondered whether he did not understand far more than I had thought possible, whether he had, in his own fashion, found the secret to prayer and the true meaning of the religious experience. I recalled a beautiful story told about the saintly founder of the Hasidic movement in Judaism, the Baal Shem Tov and the boy with the whistle.

A villager, who year after year prayed in the Baal Shem's house of prayer on the Days of Awe, had a son who could not even grasp the shapes of the Hebrew letters, let alone the meaning of the holy words. On the Days of Awe his father left him home. But when he was thirteen, he took him along on the Day of Atonement for fear the boy might eat on the fast day simply because he did not know any better.

Now the boy had a small whistle which he always blew when he sat out in the fields to herd the sheep and the calves. He had taken it with him in the pocket of his smock, and his father had not noticed it. Hour after hour, the boy sat in the house of prayer and had nothing to say. But when the additional service commenced, he said, "Father, I have my little whistle with me. I want to sing on it." The father was greatly perturbed and told him to do no such thing, and the boy restrained himself.

But when the afternoon service had begun, he said again, "Father, do let me blow my little whistle." The father became angry and said, "Where did you put it?" And when the boy told him, he laid his hand on his pocket so that the boy could not take it out. But now the closing prayer began. The boy snatched his pocket away from his father's hand, took out the whistle, and blew a loud note. All were frightened and confused. But the Baal Shem went on with the prayer, only more quickly and easily than usual. Later he said, "The boy made things easy for me, for he has prayed with his heart in the only way that he could."

I also remembered that story when the woman implied that perhaps the retarded of the Aurora Center need not be invited to our services every Friday night. How dare anyone be so presumptuous as to determine who can pray and who can't, who is welcome to God's house and who isn't! Judaism refers to prayer as the "worship service of the heart," and meaningful prayer can only come from a willing heart. The retarded individual's concept of God may be childish and his prayer naive, but it contains the ingredients most necessary to all prayer: desire and love, a service of the heart.

13
The Lighter Side

We got glimpses of Michael's ability to read and his love of music at an early age when everything seemed hopeless. As he matured, slowly mastering the art of communicating with others and the satisfaction of studying with teachers who loved and appreciated him, he began to break through the shell of diffidence and self-denigration and allowed us to see other facets of his truly fascinating personality.

He has a marvelous sense of humor. He appreciates broad comedy. He enjoys watching slapstick on television, the pie in the face, the pratfall, the ludicrous situation. He has a wonderful belly laugh. When something strikes him as funny, he lets go and laughs with his whole body. I enjoy watching him laugh, for he appears to have such a good time at it.

He also has a subtle wit which he uses on us as well as his teachers and classmates. Last summer Frances was driving the children to a supermarket. As she passed a truck spraying the neighborhood to kill mosquitoes, she asked what the men on the truck were doing. Without pausing to think Michael answered, "They're polluting us."

Michael is terribly uncoordinated and unathletic. This is part of his handicap. We have finally gotten him to ride a bike, but we go through a whole charade before he does it. Frances or I will say, "Michael, I want you to ride your bike around the block five times." "No," he says, "twice." We say five times again and he replies twice. Finally we say, "Michael, you're going to do it ten times." "Oh, all right," he then says in mock resignation, "I'll do it five times." We have followed some form of Levantine bargaining every time we ask him to take a ride, and he always plays his part to the hilt. He seems so solemn and earnest while he bargains and enjoys it immensely.

One day while bicycling, Michael rode through a sprinkler on our neighbor's front lawn. He came charging into our house and announced, "Mom, my clothing shrunk." Michael is a short, stout boy whose clothing never seems to fit. His pants strain at the belt and his shirt forever pops buttons. Quite obviously his clothing did not shrink, but he had seen the humor in the situation and was using it for his benefit.

Michael's teachers tell me that he will use his sense of humor on them or his classmates. He doesn't harm anyone. He is only having fun, at times in a most clever, yet natural, fashion.

I suspect he is using this sense of the absurd in part as a defense mechanism. He knows he is clumsy, he can't play games as more normal children do, and though he tries to hide his feelings I know how deeply hurt he is when someone pokes fun at him and calls him stupid or retarded. At first he used the most obvious and harmful form of self-protection— withdrawal. If we asked him to try some physical activity, he said no. When we urged him to go outside with the other children to play, he refused, banged his foot, and came inside as soon as he could. To a certain extent he still withdraws; he still says, "I can't; help me." But he has also found another defense mechanism—clowning. He will now try to get his classmates to laugh with him, not at him. Perhaps he will get the affection of his peers, something he so desperately craves by being funny.

In addition there is in his nature something that allows him to see the funny and even ludicrous side of life. George Santayana, the great contemporary American philosopher, once attempted to analyze humor:

> The world is a perceptual caricature of itself; at every moment it is the mockery and the contradiction of what it is pretending to be. But as it nevertheless intends all the time to be something different and highly dignified, at the next moment it corrects and checks and tries to cover up the absurd thing it was; so that a conventional world, a world of masks, is superimposed on the reality and perception this illusion, whilst the convention continues to be maintained, if we had not observed its absurdity.

We know children can at times see things far more clearly than adults. They have not learned the art of self-deception. To cite the example of the famous children's story, "The Emperor's Clothing," they see that the emperor is naked. Perhaps Michael, perceptually handicapped, can intuitively see his surroundings in a simple, unadulterated fashion, and is able to comment upon the absurdity in life.

Michael is far more sensitive then either Steve or Alexandra. The handicapped child is usually more sensitive. He is easily driven to tears or hurts himself more often than the other two. He is shy and timid. He cannot stand to hear discordant music or shrill noises. He will burst into tears if a record is played at the wrong speed on our phonograph.

He is also more sensitive to criticism or the danger of it, although at times he will attempt to hide it, and because of his handicap has difficulty verbalizing it.

For example, when on occasion I would drive him to class, then suggest walking him into his classroom, he would invariably say, "No! Don't come in." Or when he found me talking to his teacher, he would burst into tears. I asked him why. He was doing quite well in school. His teachers loved him and told me so. He could never explain himself, but always insisted that I not speak to the teachers or go into his classroom

One day I mentioned this to Frances over the dinner table. Steve chimed in with, "Don't you know why Michael hates to have you go into his classroom? We all hate to have our parents come into our classroom."

I had felt that way as a child, but I had forgotten the feeling or perhaps I had assumed that since I was an "enlightened" parent, my children would not be embarrassed. Michael, a particularly sensitive child, yet unable to verbalize his feelings, burst out crying. Steve simply told me his feelings.

Most children have ambivalent feelings when they see their brother or sister punished. Michael has never liked it. He feels empathy towards the one punished. He does not want to witness the hurt of others. Yet when it comes to physical pain, he can bear much more of it than the rest of the family. Recently he burned himself at school. We took him to the doctor, who was amazed at his composure, for it was a second-degree burn, which is quite painful. He cried when the doctor soaked the hand, pleading, "Please don't do it again," but when the dressing was done, he thanked the doctor and walked out. We had been advised to give him aspirin for the pain, but he never complained.

Michael is also an actor, a little ham. When he reads a book, he reads aloud and with expression. If there happens to be a conversation in the story, he changes his voice for each part. On a Saturday morning as he lies in bed, we can hear him playing various roles as he acts out his stories. Yet he cannot perform on a stage. On a number of occasions, his class has participated in various school programs. The teachers have rehearsed the plays with the children. Michael practices with the children and seems to enjoy himself. However, when he goes on stage in front of an audience, he becomes very shy and timid and cannot remember his lines. He seems small and frightened, afraid of making a fool of himself, afraid of making a mistake. The strange world is still too frightening for him.

Frances and I have often thought of what he would have been like had he been born without a handicap, had he been "normal." Would he have had this great love for beautiful music? Would he have acquired, on his own, this knowledge of

Judaism? Would he have possessed this marvelous sense of humor, the ability to see and laugh at the absurd? Perhaps this inner beauty, these unique attributes are God's compensation to him.

14
Discipline

Hyperactivity is the most obvious and disturbing aspect of Michael's brain damage. Even as an infant, he was always moving. However, we thought that he was just a very active child. How terribly mistaken we were. When the pediatrician first diagnosed his brain damage, he stressed this hyperactivity as proof of his findings. I asked, "How do you know Michael isn't normal? Maybe he's more active than the average youngster." The doctor answered, "Look at your other child. He sits with curiosity watching me examine his brother, but Michael keeps turning, grabbing instruments, running about in a senseless manner. He's not interested in anything I do."

The word *hyperactive* means abnormally excessive activity, but it doesn't begin to describe the true dimensions of the problem. One must live with a brain-damaged, hyperactive child to understand the inner turmoil in his mind, his difficulty in concentrating, the intense will power it takes to control his random wanderings. These children want to behave as any normal child. They want to learn. They want to please. This is part of the tragic nature of their fate, for they may be physically unable to control themselves.

I remember an incident that happened when Michael was three years old, shortly before we learned that he was handicapped. Frances had taken him shopping for groceries and she came home exhausted from the physical and mental strain of controlling him. He followed her into the house, ran over to the bags full of groceries, and began scattering them all over the kitchen. He picked up a carton of eggs and just dropped them on the floor. I became furious, lost my temper, and began slapping him. He started crying, screaming, banging his head on the floor. As he turned his face to me, I saw blank, uncomprehending eyes, a pleading look as if he were saying, *Why are you hitting me? I can't help it. I don't understand what I've done.* At that instant I felt certain Michael was not normal, but I thrust the idea from my mind. I was too terrified of the facts. I can recall that specific episode today, because I don't believe I have ever felt as guilty punishing a child as I did that afternoon.

When we learned that he was brain-damaged we knew of course that he couldn't control himself, but where should we go from there? The medication we tried either didn't work or depressed him. The soothing effects of listening to music gave us only temporary relief. Fortunately he had no difficulty falling asleep. Some children with his type of brain damage can't even go to sleep without first taking a sedative. However, he would wake up early in the morning and either keep waking us or run into the living room to toss around his toys, papers, books, or anything he could lay his hand on. In sheer desperation we started locking his bedroom door.

Michael's nursery school supervisor first made us realize how wrong we were. We had come to her with a specific problem in mind: his eating habits. Michael loves food. There are few things he will not eat, and he probably uses food as an outlet for his tension and nervous energy. He is also an extremely fast eater, and no doubt this too is part of his hyperactivity. At that time it was impossible to eat together with him. He sat at the dinner table stuffing himself with food, eating with his hands. After he finished what was on his plate, he grabbed any food in sight. It was senseless for us to yell at him; he simply ignored us.

"What should we do to control Mike?" we asked the supervisor.

"Rabbi, Frances, *who's boss?*" she replied. "You or this four-year-old? He understands you. He knows what you want, but as long as you let him get away with it, he's going to eat like a pig. His hyperactivity is no excuse for that kind of behavior. The next time he starts eating with his hand instead of a fork or spoon, the next time he grabs food from another plate, you say, 'Mike, if you do that again I'm going to take away your plate and you won't have anything to eat.' As soon as he learns you mean business, he'll follow orders. He's not going to starve. He has enough fat on him already. And he isn't going to want to be hungry. Remember, you are doing this for his sake as well as your own. He's a pathetically confused youngster. He wants and needs to be controlled. He must be taught self-control so he can function as a civilized human being. He desperately needs discipline. You, his parents, will have to provide it."

We returned home that day determined to follow her instructions. We sat down to eat our dinner. Of course Michael started to gobble his food and reach for more. I pulled his plate away and told him that he couldn't eat unless he controlled himself. He started to scream and cry. I returned his plate, and once again he began to grab for food. This time I picked him up and bodily removed him from the table. We concluded the meal while ignoring his tantrum. The next meal when we ate together, he started to reach for food, but I warned him; he quickly withdrew his hand. He had learned his lesson.

Sometime later we went again to the nursery school to discuss a problem with the supervisor. Michael was playing with a few other children in the adjoining room. When he heard our voices, he ran into our room. She ordered him to return to his class. He did, but a minute later he ran back to us. This time she said, "Michael, you go back into your room and sit in the corner chair until you think you can play with the other children and not disturb our conversation." We glanced into the other room and were flabbergasted to see Michael sitting docilely in the chair waiting for the teacher to allow him to join the other children. Was this our child? We had never seen him so quiet. "Yes, that's Michael," she assured us. "He knows who is boss in this nursery and he is going to follow my orders."

Discipline! This was the name of the game. Though we had an abstract idea of its importance, we had never applied it to Michael. As newlyweds possessing a certain cockiness and the inexperience of the young, we took for granted the fact that we would make good parents. We held certain preconceived notions about raising and educating children. We would use the most modern technique and be Spock-oriented. There would be no generation gap between us and our children as there had been between our parents and ourselves. Three of them were immigrants, and though Frances' father was born in New York City, he was middle-aged when he married, a chivalrous, kind, gentle, old-fashioned person completely dominated by his wife, with little authority in his home and over his children. My parents spoke only Yiddish to me because it was the easiest way for them to communicate, while my mother-in-law spoke a poor English with a thick accent.

I can't recall my father ever hitting me. He left that form of punishment to my mother, but he was quite capable of showing his displeasure by ignoring me. He would punish me by withdrawing his love. My parents succeeded in instilling within me a deep sense of guilt. I felt that if I didn't behave properly they would be angry and not love me.

Frances, on the other hand, was raised in a much more permissive atmosphere. Her father, being such a gentle soul, never laid a hand on her; her mother, who was the domineering personality in the family, had no idea of how to discipline her. Either she pulled her hair, chased her around the kitchen with a broom, or lay down in bed crying that Frances was making her ill and killing her. Our model for effective parenthood was certainly not our own parents. Yet how immature we were to believe that we could close the generation gap simply by speaking proper English and renouncing the examples our parents had set for us!

We had an added emotional problem in trying to discipline Michael. How do we punish a child for doing something that really isn't his fault and which he can't control? How effective could punishment be if he has no comprehension of the reason he is being punished?

The nursery school supervisor radically changed our thinking and, of course, she was right. If we are firm, Michael will listen. We were able to check his horrible eating habits and other extreme manifestations of wildness. We found that the most effective technique is to force him to sit quietly in a chair as he had done that morning at school. We designated a specific seat at home which we called the "cooling-off seat." We didn't want to use the term "bad-boy seat" because of its negative connotation. He wasn't a bad boy; only his action at that specific time was wrong. Before we let him get off the "cooling-off seat," he had to tell us why he was punished. We wanted to be quite certain that he understood what he had done that was wrong and that he would not get away with it again. We have found this technique equally effective with our other children.

We also soon learned that discipline, to be effective, has to be consistent. All children are constantly testing their parents, probing to find how far they can go before they will be stopped. Only consistent firmness will teach them "This far and no further." This certainly applies to the hyperactive, brain-damaged child such as Michael, who may easily become confused when his same action results in our punishing him one time and ignoring him the second.

Michael lives in a chaotic world, made more so by his perceptual difficulties and the turmoil in his mind. It becomes imperative, if he is ever to function as a human being, to help him create some order in his life by setting bounds for his actions. There are limits past which he may not move.

126

We were proud of ourselves one morning when the supervisor used our work as an example for the mother of another hyperactive child who was in Michael's nursery school class. "But you don't understand. He is so wild that I can't go out for an hour without taking him. I can't even leave him with a baby-sitter. I don't know what to do," the mother said.

"Why don't you follow the example of the Agress family," replied the supervisor, "and let him know who is boss, that you won't tolerate such behavior, and that he better learn to stay with a baby-sitter without taking the house apart."

Needless to say, we have put our experience with Michael to good use in our disciplining Steve and Alexandra. Children, all children, normal as well as handicapped, must know that they will be punished by their parents when they overstep permissible bounds. This is the only way that a child can feel secure in our very insecure world, and this sense of security is vital to his emotional development and well-being. Our youngsters aren't angels. They can be quite mischievous, but they know how far they are permitted to go.

When we first married, we talked of being pals and confidants to our children. We hoped they would feel so familiar with us that they could bring any problem they had to us. Subconsciously we were expressing our own childhood wishes. We loved our parents, but never felt close to them. There were no bonds of understanding, no sense of companionship between our parents and ourselves. We had missed this and wanted to make certain our children would never have that feeling. We were not about to stress discipline.

The book of Proverbs warns, "He that spareth his rod hateth his son; but he that loveth him chasteneth him betimes" (13:24). The permissive parent does not prove his love by permitting his child to set his own rules and do whatever he wants. He may be proving to his youngster that he doesn't really care for him, or that he doesn't want to be bothered by him.

We hope that our children will feel that they can come to us with their problems and be close to us. We may or may not be pals, but I pray to God that we are good parents.

Odyssey—Part Two

15
After the Grove School

The eighteen months Michael spent in the Grove School were wonderful ones. He found people who loved him, classmates he could haltingly relate to, and a positive classroom environment. Every school day morning he awoke eagerly anticipating his school, his friends, and his work, especially if it had to do with reading.

I rejoiced in his progress. He had started to use words, even though he could not speak sentences. He took great pride in his ability to read trisyllabic words, even though he did not understand them. Above all, he was far more controllable. His hyperactivity could be contained. I did not have to slap him to get his attention. Emotionally he responded to outward show of affection. He no longer screamed when I tried to hold and hug him.

But it was becoming increasingly difficult for Frances and myself to maintain the daily driving regimen. She had become pregnant in September and was due in early June. She, as always, enjoyed a good pregnancy with very little nausea or other side effects, and so was able to do her share. However, by the end of April, I did all the driving, and it was taking a toll of me, both physically and emotionally. I was perpetually tired and felt that my work as a rabbi was beginning to suffer.

131

By the middle of May we began to discuss Michael's future schooling. I did not want Frances driving to and from the Grove School with an infant the following September. I would, therefore, have to drive five days a week. Could I physically do this? Yet how could we take Michael out of the Grove School? Where would we go?

We told Virginia Matson of our dilemma. Originally we hadn't tried to have Michael placed in the Aurora public school system in one of their Educable Mentally Handicapped classes because he could not behave in a classroom. Now we wondered whether the year and a half at the Grove School had prepared him sufficiently for a public school class. "Yes," Mrs. Matson advised, "he's almost seven years old, and he's ready for regular school work. Just be careful that the public school supervisors don't try to give you a raw deal by putting him into a Trainable Mentally Handicapped class." (Children in T.M.H. classes have lower IQs than E.M.H. students. E.M.H. pupils are taught to read and to work simple arithmetic problems. An attempt is made to teach them standard elementary school work at a slower pace and simpler level. Occasionally, some of these children, if they show sufficient aptitude, are then promoted to a normal class. T.M.H. children are trained in simple chores and are not expected to do academic work.)

"Michael," Virginia continued, "is capable of doing academic work and he would be terribly misplaced in a T.M.H. class. In fact, I've had one of our youngsters leave our school, enter a T.M.H. class, and regress. While he was with us, he spoke. Once he spent time in the T.M.H. class, he stopped speaking. Make sure that Michael gets a proper education. Watch over him, and God bless you in your decision."

Yet it remained a hard decision to make, and so we decided to seek a further evaluation of Michael's capabilities. A physician friend of mine suggested a noted pediatric neurologist at one of the better Chicago hospitals. We followed the familiar procedure of contacting the hospital, sending all the data we had, including IQ tests, teacher evaluations, and the results of the various physical and neurological examinations, including the EEG. We went to the doctor's office anticipating that he would ask to see Michael and perhaps even hospitalize him while he went through an additional battery of tests. We hadn't even taken Michael along; we assumed this would be the first of a number of visits. I am usually very nervous on the night before I visit a doctor, but on this occasion, I thought, *He's not going to tell me anything, so why be anxious?*

We were surprised when the doctor began: "I've looked over you son's records and tests and I really don't think there is any reason for you to bring him for more testing. We can take a new EEG since he hasn't had one for more than two years. But I don't believe we will find anything new. EEGs aren't all that accurate. I'll bet that we'll get an abnormal reading on fifteen percent of the people who have absolutely nothing wrong with them or at least don't seem to have anything wrong with them. The readings on children are even more erratic.

"Michael is brain-damaged. If it's any consolation to you, I have never seen a hyperactive child of this sort remain that way into adult life. What are his potentialities? How far will he go? I don't know. I think the question really is, will he be able to live by himself, and this I can't answer. Only time will tell.

"Now, may I give you a bit of advice? There is a great temptation among parents of handicapped children to live only for that child. You have each other. You have other children and they are also entitled to a father and a mother. It isn't fair for any parent to sacrifice the rest of the family for the sake of one person."

All this was said calmly, with a sense of authority. "Have you ever heard of the Grove School? And should we take him out of that school and put him into the Aurora school system?" we asked.

"I've heard of the Grove School and Mrs. Matson," he replied, "and though I haven't visited the school and cannot give you the benefit of my own observations, the reports I've gotten have been good. As to transferring him to the Aurora school, I don't know what kind of program they have, but eventually he will have to leave the Grove School and make his way. I don't see why it shouldn't be at this time."

With that we concluded the interview. He had raised no hopes, except for his comment on hyperactivity, but neither had he shattered any expectations. Most of all, the advice he had given us about "not sacrificing the whole family" had made sense. Could we continue driving Michael to the Grove School, thereby endangering our own health and well-being? The following year Michael would go to the Aurora schools. In the back of our minds we believed that should this not work, we could take him back to the Grove School. He was always welcome there.

The Aurora director of pupil personnel interviewed Michael and agreed to put him in an E.M.H. class the following September. The future looked hopeful. Frances had given birth to a baby girl, Alexandra, and a school was available in Aurora for our son.

Once again, however, we were in for a rude shock. On the afternoon of the very first day, the director called us. "Michael presented problems for the teacher. He was disruptive. He didn't sit still. He didn't pay attention. She had to devote a good deal of her time and attention to him. Perhaps if he stayed for an hour in class while his mother was also in the room, he would quiet down. With time and improvement Michael can stay longer."

We, of course, complied, and for a month Frances served as Michael's baby-sitter. He didn't improve, and after the month's trial his teacher insisted that he leave her class.

The director, who was in an awkward situation, wanted to help, yet felt he could not refuse the teacher's request. He took Michael out of class and arranged that the school board pay a special tutor for an hour a day. In order to give Michael the opportunity to socialize, he also proposed that he go every after-

noon from one to three P.M. to a special, privately run but
publically supported school for retarded children. Since he was
also staff psychologist for this school, this could be arranged.
We agreed, both to the tutor and to the school.

I have often thought of Michael's first teacher in the E.M.H.
class and my attitude toward her. I disliked her, which I
imagine was to be expected. She had refused to keep him as a
pupil. He was too much trouble for her; I resented that. Her attitude reminded me of other responses when I first searched for
a school. Her position had not been unusual. It was Virginia
Matson and the Grove School that had been extraordinary.
But the Grove School had accepted him, and if they had found
him loving, controllable, and educable, why couldn't she control him? Why couldn't she respond to him in the same
manner?

She was not a completely cold, unfeeling teacher. On the
contrary, she seemed quite conscientious. Once when I was
speaking to her in the corridor of the public school, two little
girls ran up to her, grinning broadly, shouting "Hi!" and telling
her how proud they were of their marks in the third grade. They
had been students of hers in the E.M.H. class the previous year.
She had worked with them and had been able to get them into a
normal class. They liked her and appreciated all she had done
for them. The problem was that she wanted to teach a class,
and Michael was disrupting the class. He was demanding too
much of her time.

As I look back upon my contact with the various teachers in
the Grove School and examine the standards and qualifications Virginia Matson set for her staff, I realize that Michael's
teacher in the E.M.H. class, as competent and correct as she
was, did not truly qualify to work with handicapped children.
It seems to me that one must be a special sort of person to teach
exceptional children.

She must love children, in particular crippled, handicapped,
difficult, abnormal children. The special-education teacher
must be a visionary and a missionary, striving for the moment

when this abnormal child will behave as close to normal as is humanly possible, and be terribly disappointed if this doesn't happen. Each child is a challenge to this type of teacher, and the teacher will find herself going home after a day in the classroom bothered by his problems, thinking up new techniques of controlling, of helping this particular child. Special courses given in various colleges will not necessarily produce such teachers; only a commitment to an ideal, plus a love for children who need all the love they can get, will suffice.

This teacher was not an ogre. She wanted to do a competent job, but she did not have the dedication to an ideal that truly marks the special teacher of special children. She had a course of instruction to follow and a class to control. Michael took up too much of her time, required too much effort, and so he had to go.

The rest of the year was an almost complete loss for Michael. The tutor hired by the public school to work with him one hour a day was a genial, yet largely ineffectual person. She genuinely liked Michael but could not control him. She attempted to spend half an hour a day on motor coordination and the other half on academic subjects, reading, writing, and some counting games. When Michael finds something difficult or not to his liking, he becomes balky and stubborn. She tried to break down his stubbornness, but instead ended by giving in to him.

The school for the retarded to which he went in the afternoon was a waste of time and may in fact have been harmful. The purpose of his going had ostensibly been to help him socialize with children his own age. However, the retarded children at this school could not speak and hardly played with each other. Not only did Michael not learn to play with these children, but Frances and I began to note that he was using fewer and fewer words. We did not want to pull him out of the school on our own accord and in the middle of the semester, but we were determined that he would not return the following September.

One particular incident convinced us that this was not the school for him. Neither Frances nor I had visited a classroom to watch a class in action before we put him into the school. This had not been our choice. We wanted to see the school functioning, but we were told that this was against its policy. "It would be particularly disturbing to retarded children if strangers walked in or looked in their classrooms," the school administrator said. I have since become suspicious of such excuses, as plausible as they may sound. I have begun to suspect that parents looking into classrooms may be far more disturbing to teachers or administrators than to students. Parents may see things that are not too flattering. The Grove School never had such a rule. We were gladly shown the classes in sessions. The doors were always open and the students or teachers never seemed disturbed by our presence.

However, on a day in May, three weeks before school concluded, all the parents were invited to the school to see their children in action and speak to the teachers. Michael had never talked to us about the school or told us what he did there. Now at least Frances (I was busy that particular afternoon) could have some idea of what his activities were.

She returned home stunned. "All they did for three-quarters of the time I was in the classroom," she said, "was to cut strips of paper. And just before they left, the teacher collected all the strips and threw them into the wastepaper basket. The children didn't even have the satisfaction of knowing that their work was in any way useful."

I was dumbfounded. Perhaps Michael had the misfortune of having a poor teacher. Neither Frances nor I have ever spoken to the administrator about this, but I now think that we were wrong in not asking questions or determining the facts. The other parents of children going to the school seemed satisfied, at least outwardly. We were resolved not to let Michael return.

I have found, in general, that the majority of the schools and institutions for the mentally retarded are governed by the thinking of a bygone era. Tragically, a few of them are little better than eighteenth-century bedlams or snakepits, overcrowded, unsanitary, and inhuman. Others, though operated on humane principles, function essentially as custodial schools. The retarded are kept busy and taught some simple tasks. The teacher is a specialized baby-sitter. The school Michael went to, it seemed to me, was just such a custodial school. Most of the parents, thinking that their poor, retarded children were receiving humane treatment, were satisfied.

They did not realize that the school's ideas were wrong and were harming their children. Most retarded children, except for those severely handicapped, can be taught far more than these types of custodial schools are teaching. By limiting the scope of their instruction, by narrowing their horizons, they are actually hindering the possible maturation and development of the retarded. So much more could be done for the handicapped and retarded boys and girls if the community would stop thinking of them as freaks or poor, helpless souls. Many more retarded could live a useful and productive life than actually do.

16
Two Unusual Teachers

The year had come and gone. Michael had been with a teacher who barely tolerated his presence in class, an ineffectual tutor, and a school for the retarded. He was twelve months older, but he had shown very little emotional or intellectual growth. Fortunately, he had not retrogressed.

It had been a disappointing year, even a discouraging one, but the despondency that had gripped me for the 2½ pre-Grove School years did not return. I knew there was a Grove School and that, as a last resort, Michael could return there.

Most comforting of all, I believe, was a feeling that I was no longer alone, that God was near me and He would answer me. I could become discouraged, I could be angry at Michael's E.M.H. teacher or disappointed at the school for the retarded, but I need not feel hopeless. I could face the new school year realistically, determined that Michael receive the best educational opportunities available in the Chicago area.

The director of pupil personnel had promised the previous June that Michael would once again be put into an E.M.H. class, this time however with a different teacher. The first week of September he called me into his office.

"We're going to try Michael in another school." There is no central school for all E.M.H. children in Aurora. He had

139

initially been put into an elementary school two miles away. The change would mean that he was much closer to home. "We have a new special-education teacher for that particular E.M.H. class, and I want to give her a chance to get used to the other children, so we'll keep him out of school for the first two weeks. Then we can start him slowly, an hour his first week, an hour and a half his second. Maybe at the end of a few months he will be going for half the day. Let's bring him in next week so that the teacher can meet him."

I didn't particularly like the proposal. It sounded like a repetition of the previous year. Once again he would be on trial. If his behavior did not conform to the teacher's standards, he would be out. I could understand the expulsion of a youngster from class if his continued presence made teaching impossible, but this form of "on trial" gave Michael's teacher a chance to oust him as soon as he annoyed her or disturbed the class. And Michael *was* hyperactive; he *could* be disturbing; he *did* demand more attention than the normal child.

I decided I would go along for a time with the request. I sympathized with the director's position and felt he wanted to help Michael. If after a few months Michael was not attending school on a regular basis I would apply as much pressure as I possibly could.

I recall quite vividly my first meeting with the new teacher. Classes had not started when, with Michael in tow, I walked into the empty room that was to be his new classroom. She was an attractive young lady with striking blue eyes and jet black hair. She wore the brightest orange dress I had ever seen.

As I entered the room, she was in an animated conversation with the director. She introduced herself as Rela Peeler and said that she was looking forward to teaching Michael. I had planned to go on the offensive and show her I would not allow Michael to be pushed around. I immediately started the interview by telling her about his misadventures the previous year, the fact that last year's teacher had not been willing to work with him, and that I was *sure* this year would be different.

140

Rela promptly answered, "Rabbi Agress, I have been teaching special education for a number of years and I have handled difficult children before. I am quite sure that I shall know what to do with Michael."

At this point the director stepped between us and outlined his suggestions. The first few weeks Michael would be going to class an hour a day. After a certain trial period Mrs. Peeler and he would evaluate his progress and make a decision. The meeting ended shortly, and we left with a handshake and a hope that it would be a productive year.

"What do you think of her?" Frances asked as soon as I stepped into the house.

"I really can't say. She is certainly different from last year's teacher. She has her own set opinions, and I can't see anyone budging her. Only time will tell how she takes to Michael and whether he can stay in class. But I sure felt stupid trying to lay down the law to her and she put me in my place."

The following week Frances began driving Michael to school. She brought him at nine A.M. and took him home an hour later. The first day, I called home as soon as she returned to find out what had happened. Had Mrs. Peeler said anything?

"No. All she said was, 'Michael's doing fine and I'll see him tomorrow.' "

This wasn't very comforting. The E.M.H. teacher last year had also kept reassuring us with such words as "he's doing fine" and then suddenly dropped the bombshell by telling the director that she wanted him out of her class.

Every morning for a week I called Frances, and every morning Frances told me Rela Peeler had said the same thing: "He's doing fine. I'll see you tomorrow, Mike."

Friday morning Frances answered excitedly, "Mrs. Peeler told me that next week Michael will be going for the whole session. She said, 'Why don't you make arrangements with the school administration to have him bused to and from school? All our children come and go by bus. I think he will enjoy going to school for the whole day.' " This was an understatement. He loves going to school.

The year's odyssey was over. Michael was back in class. He had found a teacher who accepted him. He had found an environment similar to the Grove School. My prayers had been answered.

Rela Peeler is a most unusual teacher and a remarkable human being. She has the idealism of a dedicated special-education teacher and is able to communicate this spirit not only to the parents and the school administration, but to the students as well. She loves her students and uses her fertile imagination to devise the most unusual, yet vital, educational techniques. Even the brightly colored dresses she wore were for a reason. She pinned a tag on her dress with the name of the color written out so the children might learn to identify the different colors. She involved herself in the lives of her students, their homes as well as their school activities.

A disproportionate number of children from minority groups, blacks and Spanish-speaking, are in the E.M.H. classes. There are probably a multitude of reasons. These children are culturally deprived; they may never have seen a book or a newspaper at home. Children from Spanish-speaking homes often know very little English before they enter the public school system. There is little, if any, learning motivation at home. No doubt the IQ scores and their work in classrooms mirror this deprivation. Since they can not keep up with normal class work and may also have behavioral problems, they are taken from their classrooms and dumped into E.M.H. classes.

A number of these children come from very poor homes. It can get very cold in Aurora during winter (below zero is not uncommon), yet many wear the skimpiest of clothing in the bitterest days of winter: torn shirts and sweaters, no warm overcoats, nor galoshes over their shoes. I doubt whether they eat breakfast before they come to school. How is it possible for such children, hungry, cold and sick, to do much schoolwork?

Two Unusual Teachers

I don't know whether Mrs. Peeler approved or disapproved of her E.M.H. class being a catchall for various problem children—deprived, emotionally disturbed, slow, or partially retarded—but she was determined to help all of them. I never did learn her secret, but she had requisitioned a small second-hand refrigerator and stove for her classroom. Using federal funds for school luncheons, she had also obtained a daily pint of milk per child, cans of Campbell's soup, spaghetti, and frankfurters one day a week. Every day at 11:45 A.M. the children would put away their books and begin to prepare a hot luncheon. Each child had his or her own prescribed job. One would set the plates, a second the silverware, a third would open the cans, a fourth would help cook. Michael was perennially on K.P. Since we keep kosher at home, maintaining the Jewish dietary laws and eating only certain foods prepared in a specific fashion, Michael did not eat the hot meal. Frances sent him to school with a sandwich, but he did have the milk and eat the cooked vegetables that were frequently prepared by the "chefs" of the E.M.H. class.

Rela was accomplishing two things with these hot luncheons. All the children were learning to perform daily chores, to become self-reliant, and to learn how to eat properly. These were things Michael badly needed to learn. And all the children were at least getting one nutritious hot meal and a pint of milk a day.

Thanksgiving turned out to be a special treat. I don't know how Rela did it, but she got a turkey, which she prepared at home. On the Wednesday before Thanksgiving she brought it to school with cranberry sauce and the trimmings. The children had made costumes; some were dressed as Indians, others as Pilgrims. Benches and tables had been set up in the school playground, and all the children sat down together for a Thanksgiving dinner. The children in the normal classes at the school were fascinated by the sight and envied Michael's E.M.H. class.

After the first few months, Rela Peeler undertook the task of

143

visiting every student's home so that she might meet with the parents, discuss their children's progress, and perhaps gain some insights into the particular emotional problems of each child. I don't know how effective these meetings were, but I do know how shocked and saddened Rela was by the extremely destitute conditions of some of the families. She then began a campaign to obtain as much food and clothing as possible for Thanksgiving and Christmas so that some of these deprived children and their families could enjoy a happy holiday.

The following year, when Michael was nine, Mrs. Peeler's E.M.H. class as well as the other E.M.H. elementary grade classes were transferred to a new school with specially equipped classrooms. Under Rela's prodding a team-teaching technique was to be tried. The first three classes combined, and the three teachers worked in unison. Michael had made progress during the first year with Mrs. Peeler and she felt that she should continue to work with him for the following year.

Mrs. Peeler was joined by a second extremely fine teacher, Mrs. Nancy Auth. Although Nancy does not have the sheer stamina and energy of Rela, she is as devoted to the well-being of the children and will use her imagination to stimulate them. They complemented each other's activities beautifully, helping to create an imaginative classroom atmosphere that excited the children and made them love school.

It was during this second year that I became involved in the problems Rela and Nancy encountered as they worked to help their handicapped pupils.

One day Michael brought home a note asking all parents of E.M.H. children to attend a general meeting the following Thursday evening. There would be a panel of three special-education teachers and three parents who would discuss the problems of raising an exceptional child. I hesitated. Once again the same old emotions began to return. How could I go to such a meeting and talk to total strangers about my child? Obviously I still had not completely conquered my sense of shame. Had I been invited to such a meeting when I first learned of his handicap, I don't believe I would have gone. I would have rationalized my refusal, but the underlying reason would have been shame and a sense of isolation. Thank God, I had changed, and though I spent a restless night, I went. It was a successful meeting, well-attended with an animated, though occasionally rambling, discussion. I was quiet, held back, and didn't take part in the discussion. Toward the end of the session, one of the parents suggested that perhaps we form a special P.T.A. organization of parents with E.M.H. children. These parents had never had their own P.T.A. As parents we had little say in the regular school P.T.A., and the problems of the E.M.H. children and the normal youngsters in each school were quite different.

Rela, who was one of the organizers of the meeting as well as chairman, asked for volunteers to sit on a committee and look into the feasibility of creating such an organization. I volunteered for this committee, though I still can't explain why. At the initial meeting I was nominated for president, and at the general meeting elected.

The most important project we undertook, both in the first and second year, was the sponsorship of a summer school program for the E.M.H. elementary school children. Rela had organized and supervised such a program while teaching in Plainfield, a city some thirty miles south of Aurora. The class had met in a public school in Plainfield for the first four weeks in July, five mornings a week from nine to eleven-thirty. The time was used solely for study, reading, writing, speech, and arithmetic. E.M.H. children are slow to learn and quick to forget, and she wanted to spend some time working with them so that they did not forget over the summer and perhaps would even forge ahead.

She had obtained the use of the classroom and had personally solicited Plainfield merchants and organizations for money for tuition and school supplies. She did not want to charge the children or their parents anything. Even when she transferred to the Aurora school system she maintained the summer school in Plainfield for a year. She asked us if we wanted Michael to attend, and of course we said yes. We paid tuition for him, since he was not part of the Plainfield school system.

Every morning Rela drove him to school and at noon brought him back. The summer school sessions were beneficial to him and helpful to us. He had no children to play with at home, and he looked forward to being with these children every morning.

I therefore proposed that we sponsor such a summer school program for the coming year in Aurora. I felt certain that the Aurora school system would give us the use of two classrooms and that our organization could raise the funds to pay for two teachers, Rela and Nancy, plus any necessary school materials.

We decided that to be successful we must raise $1,200. We began appealing for funds to various manufacturers, banks, and service clubs in the community. As president I was asked to speak to these clubs and explain the needs of our summer school program and invariably the nature of our children's handicaps. I was happy to make use of this opportunity and try to help these people understand them. Invariably someone in the audience asked. "Aren't these children all alike? They all have that look." I then tried to explain the different forms of brain damage. "I don't believe you could pick one of these children out of a larger group of normal children and identify them as brain-damaged or different. When these children become confused, they may have a blank look, but wouldn't we all look stupid if we sat listening to a physicist explain Einstein's theory of relativity? These children may not be what we would call normal, but they have great potential for living a useful life, and they are special."

I found I could speak of my child as well as all the children in the E.M.H. class honestly and movingly and that I could ask for help without any sense of shame. I am happy to write that no service club ever refused to contribute. I don't think we fully appreciate how generous Americans are and how kind we can be if we understand the need and become personally involved. We were successful in raising the money, enabling our children to attend school for six weeks during the summer, reinforcing their studies and socializing with their friends. The three hours per day the children spent in summer school was the equivalent of a full day of normal school attendance, since the various extras such as gym and art were eliminated.

The meetings with my officers together with Rela and Nancy afforded me a wonderful opportunity to get to know these two marvelously dedicated teachers. I was constantly delighted at their resourcefulness. I was also shocked and surprised at the difficulties they encountered from some of the school administration.

Rela's former principal had in fact made life miserable for her and the E.M.H. children. The school was located in a middle- and upper-middle-class, almost lily-white neighborhood. The principal thought of himself as the guardian of middle-class sensibilities. These retarded children, largely from low-income minority groups, were not his clientele. He seemed to want to isolate them from the rest of the school. The newest desks and chairs were reserved for the normal classes; the E.M.H. class had to do with secondhand furniture. He objected strenuously to Rela's hot meals, but Rela wouldn't give in. At first he refused to allow the E.M.H. children to sit in on school assemblies, although they were usually better behaved than the other children. Rela finally forced him to change that rule. The E.M.H. class was the last to use the gym or other facilities. It almost seemed as if the principal were afraid that contact with these handicapped children would "contaminate" the others.

The principal at the new school was more enlightened, but he still usually ignored the needs of the E.M.H. classes unless they were forcibly drawn to his attention. He also tried to supply the E.M.H. classes with secondhand furniture. Fortunately, the school caretaker liked Rela and her handicapped students and moved new furniture into the classroom.

One particular incident, however, truly shocked me. The E.M.H. class was putting on a Christmas play for their parents. The play had gone well; the children had performed, sung, danced, and spoken their lines. Had one not known better, he would have assumed that these were normal children staging their annual Christmas play.

The children took their curtain calls, and Frances, Steve, Alexandra, and I went back to the classroom to congratulate Rela, Nancy, and Michael. As we stepped into the corridor, we noticed a commotion. One of the children had obviously become sick. As Rela told me, this child was an epileptic and had been standing backstage when she had a seizure. The other children were not particularly disturbed by it. Rela and Nancy knew exactly what to do for the child, but the principal panicked.

It is perhaps understandable that an adult who has never witnessed an epileptic seizure might be distraught and even frightened. What was not understandable and inexcusable was the order he gave Rela: "I never want that girl to participate in a play again." He was afraid this poor youngster would have an epileptic fit while on stage. This supposedly modern, specially trained individual entrusted with the education of young children would penalize and shame an innocent child because of a physical ailment over which she had no control. If these men represent the attitude of people in general toward the handicapped, then society still has an enormous distance to go before it can hope to adequately cope with the problems of the physically handicapped or mentally retarded.

I found that the parents' organization could be effective in helping Rela and Nancy fight the hardened bureaucracy of the school system and the indifference of some administrators and teachers. Rela once told me that she could usually get quick action from her principal or director by threatening to tell Rabbi Agress!

I received invaluable help from a prominent family who had a child in Michael's class and were as interested as I in the proper education of the E.M.H. children. The mother, a native-born Auroran and the daughter of a noted attorney, had very influential friends and acquaintances in Aurora. They were most instrumental in raising the funds for the summer school project. She also had a very low regard for the school bureaucracy and could always be counted upon to do battle for the teachers and the children.

Michael spent three years in the E.M.H. classes of Aurora, two with Mrs. Peeler, the third with Mrs. Auth. It seemed to me that he had made great strides during those years. He became far more manageable, learned to sit in class and be a part of the classroom environment, kept up his interest in reading, and began to study simple arithmetic. Above all, he was in a classroom with teachers who loved him and found him a challenge, worked with him, and enjoyed his pixy sense of humor.

Two months before the end of Michael's third year in the E.M.H. class, Nancy Auth, together with a young woman who was the staff psychologist, came to our home with a proposal. "The school year is drawing to a close," Nancy began, "and we have been giving Michael and his future a good deal of thought. As you know, his IQ scores are low, but Rela, the psychologist, and I all feel that he has far more potential than he shows. Unfortunately, I really haven't been able to tap this potential. The E.M.H. classes are large—fifteen children to a teacher—and it doesn't allow me to work as intensively with Michael as I want. And of course the class itself is a mixture of various types of problem children. Some of them are slow intellectually, others come from deprived homes, while a few are children with deep emotional problems. Michael needs remedial work that we can't give him; for example, he works with the speech teacher only twice a week for twenty minutes at a time. He needs far more work on his speech. He needs more

149

work on motor activity skills, and we can't help him in that area."

"You also may not be aware of the fact," the school psychologist continued, "that the legislature in Springfield recently passed a far-reaching education bill. According to this law, every community is responsible for educating the children of the community, including retarded and handicapped. If the community feels that it can't properly educate a specific problem youngster, and the child can get better training in a private school, then the state will pay up to $2,000 per school year toward the education of this child.

"We recently visited a private school up in Dundee. It's called the Summit School, and it seemed to us that they were specifically geared to work with children such as Michael. Their classes are small, no more than six youngsters to a class, and all the teachers are specially trained with master's degrees in special education. They have a speech therapist on the premises every day, and they work with the youngster's motor activities as well as classwork. They will take only those children with an average or above-average intelligence who cannot function in public school because of serious learning disabilities.

"We think Michael fits this classification and that this is the school for him. We spoke to the administration and they agree with us. We will forward the papers to the Summit School and to Springfield for the necessary $2,000, and we don't believe there should be any difficulty getting the money."

It was an exciting piece of news. The intensified instruction might well open new vistas for Michael. I could honestly feel that everything possible was being done for him. Yet I must admit I was also scared. Michael liked the E.M.H. class and his teachers, and they in turn cared for him. How would he respond to this new school, and, of equal importance, how would the new teachers respond to him? I had grown to know and admire Rela Peeler and Nancy Auth. We had created a sort of rapport, a harmonious relationship in which all of us felt free to discuss our varied problems and suggest possible solutions. Could I create such a relationship with the Summit School staff and administration? I doubted that I could. Distance itself might well make close relationships almost impossible.

However, the move had to be made, both for Michael and our own sake.

Rela and Nancy had proven to be marvelous teachers and wonderful women. They had shown me once again, if such proof was really necessary, that the teacher is the most important factor in a handicapped child's education and that the attitude of the teacher is most vital to her educational technique. Rela and Nancy were devoted not only to our child but to all their youngsters, working for their well-being in or out of school. I shall always treasure the memory of the Thanksgiving dinner or the sight of these children acting, singing, and dancing through Christmas plays with such care and zest. I shall long remember Rela's stubborn determination to make certain her children were treated as equals.

I shall retain the knowledge that a few people working together can do many things and change attitudes even in the face of prejudices centuries old. The Parents' Organization for Special Education not only raised monies for a vitally needed summer school program and served as a forum for pressure against recalcitrant school officials, but it also fulfilled the necessary psychological and emotional role of bringing together desperate people with similar agonizing problems of handling handicapped children.

17
The Summit School

The Summit School sounded like a fine place for Michael, but Frances and I decided that one of us would visit it before we made a final decision. The school is located in a small town thirty miles north of Aurora and holds classes in a Congregational church. As I drove up to the church, memories of my first visit to the Grove School flashed through my mind.

I was immediately impressed and delighted. A sense of calmness could be felt, almost as if the serenity one associates with a house of God had become a permanent feature of this church and school.

Two of the classroom doors stood ajar. In one, about four or five boys were sitting at desks doing schoolwork. A teacher was sitting at a desk with one of the students. They seemed to be of junior- or senior-high-school age, all intently working at their specific projects. The second room appeared to be some sort of lounge where two boys were sitting at a table and playing with a hockey game while two others were playing checkers. All the youngsters were talking quietly while playing their games.

The principal, who had also been the school's founder, stepped out of her office to greet me and invited me into a large room for a chat. She explained the purpose of her school: "To work with children who have learning disabilities so that they may eventually return to the public schools and their normal public-school classes. Summit School classes meet from eight-thirty in the morning to twelve-thirty in the afternoon. Many of the pupils are then bused to their community public schools and spend some time in class with their peer group so that their eventual integration into the public-school system can be a smooth one."

She continued to explain the program, the work with a speech therapist and motor activity teacher, the intensive individual attention given to each child. "Each afternoon," she added, "our staff goes over the progress of the individual child and plans the course of study for the following day.

"You know, of course," she concluded, "that we have certain rules in our admission procedures. We do not take every handicapped child, only those with the potential of doing average or above-average work in a normal public-school class. Because of certain problems, either emotional or physical such as perceptual disabilities or brain dysfunction, these students have not been able to function properly. I have spoken with Michael's teacher and his psychologist, and they tell me that we may be able to help him. However, before we enroll him, he will have to be tested and examined by our own psychiatrist. We will base our final decision upon his judgment. Here is his phone number. Please call him as soon as you can so that we may finalize our plans for Michael."

As I left the school, I was excited and relieved. The school seemed an ideal place for eleven-year-old Michael. Although he would not be going as many hours a day, he would be receiving intensive, personalized, specialized instruction. I really did not believe he could enter a normal public-school class even for an hour, but perhaps with time, this too would occur. The principal was a most kind and gracious woman with many years of work in the field of special education and was quite obviously devoted to the betterment of her children and the selection of the most capable teachers.

One question still remained unanswered. Would the

psychiatrist qualify Michael for the school? Our experience had been that most of the professionals we consulted about Michael, the psychologists or neurologists, did not share his teacher's views that he had far more potential than his test scores indicated. Once again his future lay in the hands of a psychiatrist. I didn't want to feel discouraged but I was so afraid of hearing the doctor say, "He doesn't qualify for our program . . . ." I was anxious to have him admitted.

It's not possible to judge a school on a one-day visit, but I had had enough experience with poor schools and I thought I could easily recognize one. I recalled my first impression of the private school for the retarded in Chicago with its high wall and police dog in the lobby, or the school for the retarded Michael had attended in Aurora which refused to permit parents to see the classes in action except on a specified visitation day. I also remembered that I had fallen in love with the Grove School after spending only half an hour in the building.

Two weeks later Michael and Frances met with the doctor. After an hour's observation, he assured Frances that he would recommend him for admittance. He also suggested that we try medication. He knew Michael had been on various drugs with little appreciable gain, but there were certain differences. A good number of new drugs that had a tranquilizing effect on some hyperactive children were now on the market. He had had some successes with these drugs. Equally as important, we had never tried the drugs on a careful, qualified, experimental basis. We had never been in touch with a doctor who had wide experience using these drugs and could suggest cutting dosage or increasing it or changing prescriptions. It was worth a try, and Frances readily agreed.

Michael's admittance to the Summit School should now have gone smoothly. The Aurora school system had recommended him, the psychiatrist had qualified him, and the Summit School was happy to have him as a pupil. His prospective teacher at the school had met with him for two hours in

August, three weeks before the start of school, and found him a delightful child.

Three days before school was to start, I called to ask what transportation arrangements had been made.

"Rabbi Agress, I'm afraid I have some disturbing news for you about Michael." It was director of pupil personnel in Aurora, the person in charge of arranging for the money to come from the state. "The Illinois Department of Education doesn't want to give us the money for his tuition. They say that we should be able to educate him here."

At that moment, I had an awful sinking feeling in the pit of my stomach. *Why*, I thought, *is everything so difficult for Michael. Why can't he have the chance all other children have?* And then I became very angry.

"Do you honestly believe the Summit School offers him more than you can give him in Aurora?" I asked.

"Yes, I do."

"Well, then, I'm going to see to it that he gets that education and that tuition even if I have to drive to Springfield and camp at the Department of Education office until I get an okay from them."

I called the Summit School and told them of the situation. They would keep Michael's place available at least for the time being and told me that other parents were having the same troubles with state funds. They thought personal attention on my part might help.

I decided to contact my state representative. I had met him on a number of occasions when he either visited our temple or we were at the same social function together, but it was only a nodding acquaintance.

I went to see him on a Sunday afternoon. I told him my problem and asked him if he could help me by arranging a meeting with the man who was in charge of special education for the state. After listening to my problem, he walked over to his desk, picked up two letters, and handed them to me. They were from other parents with handicapped children also appealing for state aid.

"I'm going to Springfield tomorrow morning," he said, "and I'm going to visit the state Department of Special Education and show the director these letters. These people need my help, and I hope to God I can help them. Rabbi, you type out a letter with the details of Michael's problem and get it to me this evening and I'll take it with me tomorrow. I can't promise you results, but I'll surely try."

He hadn't asked me for any favors, or whom I had voted for in the last election, or if I would vote for him in this one. He only told me to get him the letter and he would try to do the rest.

A few weeks later, Michael's tuition grant came through, and he left the E.M.H. class to start school at the Summit School in Dundee. I shall always be grateful to this man and think of him as a prototype of a representative in a great and democratic country where an individual and his well-being is important to our government.

Every morning, Michael was taken by private taxi, paid for by both the state Department of Education and the Aurora Board of Education, to the Summit School and brought back at one P.M. We felt certain he would not be able to attend a normal public-school class even for an hour, and we were right.

We were also afraid we could not maintain the same contact with the Summit School as we had with the Grove School and the E.M.H. class; in this, too, we were correct. The school is thirty miles from Aurora, and its monthly parent-teacher meetings are held on Friday nights when we cannot attend for religious reasons. We made this clear to them, but Friday evening seemed to be the most convenient time for most parents, and so no attempt was made to change nights. For the first four months, all Michael's teacher would tell us was that his pants kept slipping down below his waist and would we please remedy it, since the other children were making fun of him.

Michael seemed to be enjoying the school; he never balked about going, but he has always been close-mouthed about his work in any school, and we learned very little of what he was actually learning or doing.

Finally we got an appointment with his teacher, and one afternoon Frances drove to the school to find out what was going on. Some five hours later she returned, exhausted.

"Will you believe it," she began, "but that woman kept talking for three hours, and if it weren't for the principal, she would still be talking. Michael's speech therapist also sat in. They both agreed that for the first few weeks, he had them baffled. They had no idea of what he could say. They thought he only knew a few words until they finally realized he was pulling their leg and could speak far better than he did. To cite an example, his speech therapist said that after class he would walk over to the coatrack, look for anyone who was nearby, point to the rack and say 'Coat.' She has now trained all the staff to ignore Michael until he asks for it and uses clear, intelligible sentences, and even then to make him try to get his coat before asking for help. The therapist is a fine teacher, and she told me that many a day she had gone home mentally taking Michael with her. She has spent nights thinking of what to do with him on the morrow so he could do his own work and not depend upon others.

"Both agreed that he must begin to grow up and start working on his own, taking care of certain responsibilities, and start relating to his classmates—in short, become a self-sufficient person, at least to a degree. He is still hyperactive, still gets up from his seat without permission and wanders around the room. She had tried something new with him by putting a sandbag on his lap as a reminder that he should not stand up. If he behaved himself on a particular day, the following day a bit of sand was removed.

"They also agreed that everyone must begin to make demands upon Michael and expect him to accomplish certain tasks. He may balk at these demands, try with all his cunning to avoid work, and expect that we, his parents and teachers, do everything necessary for him, but it is vital that we no longer coddle him."

That evening Frances and I sat down to plan how we were going to get him to follow the teacher's suggestion.

We would no longer listen to any of Michael's requests unless he used a complete English sentence. Verbal shorthand such as "Milk," "Drink," "More," "Dessert," "Change it" was out. We had made such resolutions before in the hope of forcing him to speak properly, but Michael can be stubborn, and ultimately wore away our resolve. It was easier to follow his one-word requests than to fight with him. This time we were determined not to forget or give in.

Frances also suggested that one chore Michael should be expected to do was to clear the supper dishes and dry those objects that did not go into the dishwasher—the steak knives and some of the glasses and pots and pans. At first he loved the idea. He could play waiter. But as the fun began to wear off and he realized that this was his job, night in and night out, he started dillydallying, evading work, and generally making himself obnoxious. Frances persisted and Michael continued to do the work.

The months flew by. We were told that the principal had changed Michael to a class with older children, but very little else. In the beginning of May, 1971, the principal once again called to make an appointment with us for the following Wednesday. I assumed that this time we would be discussing Michael's future plans for the following year. I was right.

Frances and I both went, leaving Michael in the care of a neighbor. The principal invited us into the lounge while she called in his new teacher. I noticed that both of them wore maroon-colored blazers with the insignia of the school on the breast pocket. Was this an attempt to add some "class" to the school?

"It is our considered opinion," the principal began, "that Michael would be better off in a school he could attend for a full day. He is making some progress, but it is slow, and as you know the goal of our school is eventually to send our children back to a public school. We have, therefore, contacted another school in Chicago that works with the same type of children as ours. We explained to them about Michael and I would suggest that you call them."

That was it! The following year he would not be returning to the Summit School. I left the school that afternoon with mixed emotions. I had been flattered by the idea that the Summit School considered him potentially bright. But he was going three hours a day, and part of the last hour was lunch period. However, he was so anxious to continue with his work that at times he would leave his sandwich untouched. This in itself was almost unheard-of, because he loves food. Finally, we had never succeeded in creating the rapport we had with his other schools, and we felt that though this school may do well with other less handicapped children, Michael had not gone as far as he should. We were not unhappy at the prospect of changing.

18
Closing the Circle

I have made it a practice to call Virginia Matson before visiting any new school. I trust her judgment completely, and she knows most of the schools in the field of special education. The Grove School had been one of the first in the state working with brain-damaged children. This was long before Illinois passed the legislation to require each school board to offer proper education to every child, including the handicapped. Since this law has come into effect, special schools have proliferated. Unfortunately they are of unequal quality. I had called her concerning the Summit School, and she had not been enthusiastic. She didn't like the idea that Michael was going only for three hours, and she didn't believe sending pupils back to public-school classes during the afternoon was effective.

"I'm glad you're not sending him back to the Summit School," Virginia said over the phone, "and I've heard of the school they recommend. It's a small school with individual attention given to each child and it could work, but if you run into any difficulty, give me a call. I may have something for you."

Ironically, I, too, had heard about the school, or rather about its founder, some years ago. It was shortly after we found the Grove School. A friend had told me that this woman was trying to start a school for children with learning disabilities, and she could use some help. I had called her, and she had sounded enthusiastic. "Fine, why don't you come up and we'll talk." The following week, I had visited her at her apartment. She was a single, middle-aged woman, lanky with a hawkish nose and a syrupy voice. She fancied herself a poet.

"Thank you for coming up," she began, "and tell me all about Michael." After I had given her all the details of his life and our struggle, she said, "He sounds like the type of youngster I want to help. I hope we can start the school in September. With your connections as a rabbi, I'm sure you can be of invaluable assistance to me." I had no intention of transferring Michael, but I knew how important such schools were and wished her well. I also said I would do all I could to help her.

Before we parted, she had said something that bothered me. She remarked, "The establishment doesn't want me to succeed." What establishment? Why were they against her?

In the intervening years I read some bits of news about her and the school she had founded. Now, five years later, I was once again calling her.

"Yes, I remember having met you, rabbi, and I think Summit School contacted us. But you must understand that we have certain rules. We don't take every child. Send us a transcript of all his records and I will call you and set up an appointment with Michael."

We authorized the Summit School and our pediatrician to dispatch the transcripts. We waited. A week passed, two, three, four weeks. July came and still no phone call. We finally decided to call ourselves. The woman replied, "I'm sorry, but we've been busy with the closing of our school year. Why doesn't your wife bring Michael to see us next week?"

Frances came home puzzled by the interview. The staff had been nice, although the assistant to the director was somewhat distant. The director, with her sweetly coy voice that Frances found irritating, kept injecting herself into the testing or rubbing Michael's back while cooing, "You're doing just fine."

"I don't know what happens now," Frances concluded. "All that woman said was, 'We'll call you later with the results.' "

Once again we waited, and as before we finally called her. "I thought I told your wife," the director answered over the phone, "that we must test Michael further. I suggest you bring him in for a few days to our summer program and let our staff evaluate him in a classroom environment." For one week we drove in with him every morning and picked him up every afternoon. On Friday I walked into the school to take him home and asked the assistant to the director what the results were. Were they going to accept him? "The director will call you. She is the only person with the authority to admit or reject a student."

We waited the entire following week with the same results—no phone call. We were in the middle of August and we had to have an answer. Applications had to be completed and sent to the state Department of Education, arrangements had to be made for transporting him to and from school. And what if he weren't accepted? We would have to repeat the whole tortuous process, the interviews, transcripts, tests. Yet school was scheduled to start in three weeks. We called again. This time the response was "The full committee hasn't met. We have our own doctor with whom we consult. You will hear from me Thursday night."

We did not hear from her on Thursday night and phoned her on Friday. "You will be happy to hear, rabbi," she began, "that we have accepted Michael on a trial basis." I didn't like the condition. I recalled the year's trial he had gone through when we first transferred him to the Aurora school system, but I didn't want to say no. Experts had recommended the school.

"You will also have to make arrangements with your school board in Aurora for his transportation," she continued. This, too, sounded peculiar, since the year before the Summit School had made the necessary contacts with the board and I assumed that was standard procedure.

"And tuition for Michael will be $3,500 a year, payable in monthly installments on the first of each month."

I couldn't believe my ears. "Why are we being charged this money when the state and the local school board pay $2,000 plus transportation toward his education?"

"The $3,500, dear rabbi, is in addition to the $2,000 we receive from the state. We have a marvelous staff which is well-paid."

This was too much. "Where am I going to get that kind of money?" I asked.

"That's too bad," she responded. "Didn't the Summit School tell you our tuition fee?" They had not.

At this point I was furious. "What kind of game are you playing with me? You know I can't meet this cost. You stall me for three months without telling me if Michael is accepted. I had to constantly call you, and now this."

"I knew you would be trouble," she answered. "I'm too busy to call everyone. As a parent, it's your job to call me. Furthermore, do you think you're the only father with a brain-damaged child?"

I couldn't say anything. Through the long years of Michael's handicap, I had never experienced such callous words. This woman was the founder and director of a special school for the handicapped. What a tragic situation for these children. I slammed down the phone, furious and sick to my stomach, and sat numbly looking at the wall.

Finally, I picked up the receiver and dialed Virginia Matson. She listened to my story and said, "We have a class for Michael. We have a good number of severely handicapped children, but we also have two small classes with boys like Mike. Now that the state will provide transportation, he can come to us."

There are a multitude of reasons why individuals start schools and homes for the brain-damaged and the retarded. Some become interested because of a personal experience in their own family. Others have an affinity for teaching special education, enjoy working with these children, and feel a sense of accomplishment in this work. A few do this out of love for the afflicted, a magnificent compassion, and a burning idealism.

Unfortunately there are those who use this type of work to compensate for their loneliness, their barren existence and neurotic tendencies. Perhaps they experience a feeling of superiority because of the influence they wield over these afflicted children and the gratitude of the parents. The schools they establish may do adequate work, but their influence can be dangerous. Parents must be on guard to recognize and resist such individuals.

In a sense, Michael had come home. He was so excited at the prospect of returning to the Grove School that for the first few nights he barely slept. Every morning at six-thirty a taxi picked him up, delivered him to a second taxi, which in turn drove him and two other children to the Grove School bus near O'Hare airport. The morning trip took $2\frac{1}{2}$ hours. The return ride was quicker since he used only one taxi and the bus, arriving home in an hour and a half. For a young boy he did a great deal of traveling everyday, but it did not seem to affect his work.

The growing-up process of teaching Michael to do his own studying and to become more self-reliant continued. The Grove School used a reward method. If Michael did good work, he received a point in his booklet. When he collected enough points, he went to the Grove School store and "purchased" with these points games or toys that had been donated to the school.

As with any attempt to change Michael, it is a slow process which he resisted every step of the way. But we saw the change: a less frequent "Help me" or "I can't do it" or "I don't know"; more self-confidence, more ease in physical work.

At one of the P.T.A. meetings I spoke to Michael's teacher. I was informed, "Mike is making good progress. I am especially pleased with his reading. He can now read a complete story and answer the questions based upon the story.

"His motor activity work is also coming along," the teacher continued. "Bill, the gym teacher, has even gotten Mike to stand and jump on the trampoline." Only a few months before, Michael had been so frightened of the trampoline that he begged us not to send him to school.

However, the teacher's final words gave me the greatest pleasure. "I feel," he concluded, "that Michael has a great deal of potential if we can only get to it and bring it to the surface. He is such a lovable child." He was echoing the sentiments of other teachers, words that have given me such joy, permitted me to hope, and maintained my courage through difficult times.

As the school year drew to a close we were once again faced with the question of what school Michael would attend for the following year. The reports from the Grove School were good. He was making good progress. He had established a fine rapport with his teacher and had continued improving in work and behavior. In fact we were swamped with games as he accumulated points. He had kept on with his gross motor skill work. However, he was spending four hours every day in a car or bus. Tuition and transportation were costing the Aurora school district far in excess of the $2,000 state reimbursement. The Aurora director of pupil personnel did not believe that the school system would continue spending such sums on one child.

Once again Frances and I visited with Virginia at the Grove School.

"Mike has been doing beautifully," Virginia explained, "and I have been sending your school system progress reports. But I can understand their problem and also the difficulty in transporting him for four hours. I have suggested meeting with the director and outlining what we have been doing with Michael this school year. There is no reason to doubt his continued progress in the Aurora public school system. I would go along with them."

Virginia had relieved our minds. She had encouraged us in

the necessary decision to transfer Michael back to the Aurora school system. She would help us make the proper adjustments.

The learning situation in the E.M.H. class of the Aurora public school is quite different from the Grove School. He is not in a class of three but of twelve. He cannot have individual attention. He must learn to work on his own and not disturb either his teacher or his class. This is one of the reasons we made the change. We felt that Michael must eventually learn to function on his own without the constant goading and encouragement of an adult. We have, therefore, established close lines of communication with the teacher. Whenever Mike becomes too rambunctious, calls out, distracts the class or refuses to do his work, the teacher writes us a note and we punish Michael by not allowing him to watch television until we get another note telling us that his behavior has improved. On the other hand, when he does good work, the teacher informs us and we reward Michael.

Progress is slow. All too frequently he sits at his desk and daydreams or does sloppy classwork, guessing at the answer without pausing to think out the problem. This is particularly so when he studies a subject he does not like or has difficulty doing. But we are encouraged by the times he turns in good work, and we sense that he is making progress, that he is learning to control himself, to work by himself, and to take pride in his work. In short, Michael is growing up and maturing.

So much in Michael's future remains unanswered. Will he ultimately be capable of caring for himself, going to work, earning money and living by himself?

Michael's mental and emotional growth has not been a matter of gradual maturation, of slow and steady progress. It has rather been a process of reaching a specific plateau, remaining on that plateau, and then spurting ahead. What lies behind these sudden spurts? Perhaps this is the way Michael's mind works, a period of maturation and learning followed by a lengthier period of ingestion and rest, somewhat similar to a tired and sick person who walks for a bit and then rests before walking again. Or perhaps the spurts are a response to some outside stimuli, a change in Michael's environment and particularly the attitudes of those around him. During this past year Michael has seemed to spurt, largely due, I think, to changes in our attitude. We expect more of Michael and are making greater demands upon him. We are forcing him to rely upon himself, and we are getting results. As he accomplishes more, his ego and self-esteem grow, and this in turn helps him do more.

Starting as a joke, I have lately labeled Michael's constructive and mature actions as the actions of the "new Michael." The "old Michael" is when he has been childish and silly. Predictably, my other children have taken to the name; Alexandra constantly asks me, "Daddy, is this the 'old Michael' or the 'new Michael'?" Michael is taking it without rancor and in a spirit of fun. At this point, however, I can't help but ask myself if I haven't hit on some truth. Perhaps this is a new Michael. I don't know, for Michael remains an enigma.

Reflections—Part Two

19
Looking Back

As a youngster, I enjoyed summer afternoons in the public library, a magnificent-looking structure three stories high, two huge front doors with sculptured figures of a distant past— Egypt, Babylon, Rome—and a marble entranceway. Even its name seemed to signify something important—The Grand Army Plaza Branch of the Brooklyn Public Library. I browsed through the shelves for hours, reading from one book, looking at the pictures of another, and finally deciding on four or five particular books to borrow and return the following week.

My reading tastes were broad and general: fiction, biographies, autobiographies, American and world histories, mysteries, and detective stories. I did have two criteria. I wanted a book, be it fact or fiction, that could carry me from the grimy Brooklyn streets and the humdrum existence of a lonely childhood to an excitingly different time and place, a heroic life. I also wanted a happy ending, the hero triumphant, the heroine saved, the final victory rousing and complete. No ambiguities for me, no indecision or questions left unanswered, no problems unresolved.

Daydreams, fantasy, heroics—all this is part of adolescence, the growing-up process, but one hopes that adulthood will produce a certain maturity, the recognition of reality, the realization that happy endings are indeed rare and that many of life's problems are neither easily nor heroically resolved.

I recall the vivid daydreams I had the first weeks following the pediatrician's initial diagnosis of Michael's condition. Frances took Michael for a battery of tests, electroencephalograms, head and skull x-rays, and blood tests while I imagined that the tests showed a tumor pressing against his brain, stopping him from speaking, making him hyperactive. I saw myself pacing the hospital corridors, waiting for word from the operating room. Would Michael live or die? All the ingredients of a fiction story were present in my daydreams: the danger, the tense waiting, the final answer, and the happy ending. Michael had been saved and would be a normal child.

The truth, of course, was far less heroic. The test results were negative. Michael most obviously had been born with this condition, hyperactive and brain-damaged. When I mentioned the possibility of a tumor to the doctor, he said we were fortunate Michael didn't have one. Otherwise, his future would have been blacker.

One of the most difficult facts for me to face was the uncertainty of Michael's future. How would he develop? Would he be able to care for himself, or would we always have to take care of him? At times I would think, "If only I knew what Michael's capabilities were," while at other times, "Please let me not know—so that I can continue to hope."

Long, emotionally wearing years have passed; years of turmoil and despair followed by hope and solace. Dreams have been shattered but self-awareness has been gained. The uncertainty in Michael's life lingers on; the future is still a great question mark; but certain events have very perceptibly changed Michael's life and radically altered mine.

They are turning points in Michael's life, and I now think of them almost as if they were miracles. Some are associated with schools to which Michael went or is still going. These schools came on the scene at the darkest of all possible moments and are indelibly etched in my memory.

The Albert Einstein Medical Center and its nursery school supervisor appeared at the depth of my despair, when all seemed lost. It was the doctors of the medical center who first held out a smidgen of hope to us that perhaps he was not unmanageable or hopeless. The supervisor was certain that he was far smarter than we assumed and that his problems were largely emotional. She insisted that he had learned to successfully manipulate us, to play us as puppets on a string.

Some of her theories sounded pretty far-fetched. How had he become so emotionally crippled, so hyperactive, refusing to speak and communicate save in the most elementary of fashions? But she did help us successfully toilet-train him, and there are times even today when Michael will do something in what seems a wholly irrational and immature manner, yet I catch a mischievous glimmer in his eye. At these moments I wonder whether Michael is not doing this to obtain some response and control over his parents. To paraphrase William Shakespeare, "There seems to be method in his madness."

Rela Peeler also came on the scene at a critical moment in Michael's development. He had been shunted the previous year between an hour a day in private tutoring and two hours a day at a school for retarded children for the purpose of "socializing." This could not continue. It was proving harmful to him and to us.

She altered this. Michael was, for the very first time in his life, a student in a public-school class. Granted, the class was an Educable Mentally Handicapped one; the number of students fourteen, large by E.M.H. standards, but small in terms of an average class; and the teacher was one of the most exceptional and outstanding in the system. Nevertheless, Michael was going to school each and every day for a full five-hour session.

Michael was learning and treasuring the experience. He was studying reading, comprehension, spelling, writing, and the start of the most rudimentary arithmetic by adding and subtracting multicolored wooden blocks. His fellow classmates liked him. On more than one occasion another youngster would come over to Michael while we were shopping in the supermarket and call out with the broadest of grins, "Hi, Mike!" Michael didn't respond. He has always been shy, but afterward, with some prodding, he would tell us the name of the boy and that he was in his class. According to Rela, Michael was sort of a class mascot and at times the class buffoon, though he knew he was serving as a buffoon. Above all, Rela loved him. No doubt at times he frustrated her, even infuriated her, but that deep affection always remained. This love enabled Michael to enjoy school, to build up some confidence in himself, some acceptance of his own worth. Although so much remained to be done, a start had been made.

Frances and I had agonized many a night over our decision to leave New York. We were certain that we would be happier in Aurora, but what of Michael? Could we find the proper medical care or schooling in a city of only seventy thousand? This decision soon turned into a blessing. We found pediatricians genuinely concerned with Michael's welfare, aware of his problems, and always prepared to spend as much time with us as was necessary. They are not only doctors but friends. Our local state representative was prepared to meet with the necessary state educational officials on our behalf. The board of education paid for Michael's tuition at a time when no state law required such payments. We have always had entree to the offices of the director of pupil personnel, the teachers and principal. Our friend and next-door neighbor is the principal of Michael's junior high school. Living in a much smaller city we are among friends, neighbors, and people who care.

And the move to Aurora brought us to the Grove School. It came into our lives on two separate occasions. It stands out in my mind as having had the greatest and most immediate impact. I heard of the school at a time of critical despair. It transformed Michael from a bewildered, wild, hurt animal into a loving, spiritually beautiful, though still handicapped child. He started to use words in a meaningful fashion for the first time in his life. Also for the first time, he experienced the feeling of being part of a class and relating to other children. The school gave him a sense of stability and continuity, the knowledge that here were people who really cared about him as a person. Most important of all, they loved him and taught him to reciprocate this love.

The Grove School also gave Frances hope. For over two years Frances had felt imprisoned by the enormity of the task facing her, the prospect of Michael being home all day, vegetating, growing wilder, less responsive, and less coherent. The school removed that fear, lightened her overwhelming burden, and gave her hope of a brighter future, of a child who would be a human being.

Equally profound were the changes going on in my mind and soul during these first few years. The dynamics of the tragedy struck me and the shattering grief and loneliness forced me to reevaluate my life, my most cherished beliefs, my pride, and the goals I had set for myself and for my children.

When Michael was still in Frances' womb, I daydreamed of my child's future. If a boy, would he follow my footsteps into the rabbinate, would he become an attorney, a doctor, or a scientist? I took for granted that he would attend college. I wanted him to be happy, but this is such a nebulous term. I had equated it with success, with material well-being. I had ignored the sage advice of ancient rabbis: "Who is wealthy? He who is happy with his portion in life."

These prideful assumptions disappeared with the words, "Michael has brain damage and may be retarded." In place of pride came an equally selfish though opposite response, self-pity. I could think only of myself, my misfortunes, my feelings. There was little, if any room in heart or mind for my wife or children as I found I was wallowing uncontrollably in a sea of despair and self-pity.

I don't think I ever really lost faith in a Supreme Deity, in the Creator of the world. I continued to function as a rabbi, preaching the concept of a personal God. Even in my darkest and most despondent days I kept reciting the daily prayers in the privacy of my home as well as at services in my temple. Some may claim all this was but a continuation of lifelong habits, but I know this is not so. A hope lingered within me, the hope that God would make His presence known to me in some fashion, at some time, in some place. So far, I had prayed to Him and He had not answered. I had prayed to hear Michael speak and he was still silent. Perhaps . . . perhaps . . . He would yet answer.

I had, however, lost all faith in others. This was a time when Michael, Frances, and I all desperately needed some help, some advice, some guidance. We hadn't the vaguest notion of what to expect, how to cope with such a predicament, such a tragedy; the people to whom we turned failed us.

The pediatrician who originally diagnosed Michael's condition was a competent but busy doctor. How much time was he expected to give the hysterical parents of a retarded child? In addition he once admitted in a moment of frustration that he had had little experience in dealing with hyperactive children, yet he never recommended that we see another, better-informed pediatrician. The neurologist was even more heartless, suggesting to Frances that Michael might well be retarded and hinting that perhaps she have another baby as soon as possible so she could forget.

The doctors at the Einstein Medical Center, his nursery school supervisor, all the hospital personnel treated us with kindness and consideration. The neurologist, a pleasant young man, spent as much time with us at the final evaluation meeting as we wanted, answering all our questions, trying to allay many of our anxieties, assuring us that Michael's brain damage was not our fault, and offering to enroll him in the medical center's nursery for further observation and some training.

Eight months of frustration in Chicago, however, made us forget all that kindness. The coldly calculated professionalism and self-assurance of the neurologist at the evaluation clinic in

Chicago had pretty well persuaded me that these doctors didn't know what they were talking about.

"Michael is retarded. Why don't you visit this school? It would be fine for him." It turned out to be an institution with an iron fence, a German shepherd dog, and basket-weaving classes.

I soon forgot the nursery school in New York and kept on hearing: "He's too hyperactive for us. Try another school."

"He doesn't fall into the category of the type of child we work with in our school. Perhaps you'll be more successful with this other school."

Everyone was trying to be "so helpful;" no one was doing a thing.

I had also lost faith in myself. If I could not cope with the problem of Michael, how could I handle any other crisis? I wavered between pity for Michael and moments of shame-filled hatred, both for my child and myself. I wanted desperately to help him, but how? I felt so terribly inadequate, so helpless, so much a nothing, a cipher, a useless being.

At this critical juncture in my life—having lost faith in others, in myself, and in the hope that God would make His presence known to me and answer me—I visited the Grove School and met Virginia Matson.

Within a half-hour, Virginia had said, "When do you want Michael to begin? We can start him today." She had also added, "I know a rabbi doesn't make a good deal of money. Whatever you two can afford to give the school will be just fine with us."

I had never hedged at the costs for Michael's schooling. If necessary I would go into debt. Michael's needs and education came first.

Yet here was a woman who had met us a brief half-hour ago and was offering to give my child the schooling he so desperately needed without any concern for financial arrangements.

Her primary concern, as she spoke to me, was neither money nor the question of whether Michael would successfully fit into the school's program. She was only interested in Michael the child. Did he need help? Then she would help him.

She is a deeply religious woman with a strong and abiding faith in God and a commanding knowledge of the Bible. Her faith, her obviously felt love of those less fortunate, the crippled in body, mind, and soul: these attitudes had a profound and lasting effect upon me.

As I drove home from the Grove School that wintery morning, the first few words of an ancient, time-honored Hebrew prayer kept running through me mind: "*Yisgadal, V'yiskadash Shemay Rabah*" ("Magnified and sanctified is the glory of God"), from the *Kaddish,* the prayer for the dead:

Magnified and sanctified is the glory of God
In the world created according to His will.
May His sovereignty soon be acknowledged
During our lives and the life of all Israel.
Let us say: Amen.
May the glory of God be eternally praised,
Hallowed and extolled, lauded and exalted,
Honored and revered, adored and worshiped
Beyond all songs and hymns of exaltation,
Beyond all praise which man can utter
Is the glory of the Holy One, praised is He.
Let us say: Amen.
Let there be abundant peace from heaven
And life's goodness for us and for all Israel.
Let us say: Amen.
He who ordains the order of the universe
Will mercifully bring peace
To us and to all Israel.
Let us say: Amen.

Why had I thought of death at this particular moment? What had death to do with Michael? What had the *Kaddish* to do with Virginia Matson or the Grove School?

Nothing and everything.

Was my shock any less at hearing the word *brain-damaged*

than receiving a telegram from Israel a year and a half later saying, "Your father just died"? Is death only a physically descriptive word? What word do we use to describe the feelings of a husband who has committed his wife to an insane asylum, or the emotions of children watching the labored breathing of a comatose father?

For that matter, what has the *Kaddish* prayer, containing no reference at all to death, heaven, hell, or the resurrection of the dead, to do with death?

The answer lay in the core of this prayer. In Judaism, on the day of burial a brief service is recited by the rabbi at the grave site. At the conclusion of this service, after the casket has been lowered into the grave, when the finality of death is so painfully obvious to all, the immediate family and those nearest and dearest to the deceased rise and say the *Kaddish*—a prayer not of death, but of its very opposite—life. "He who ordains the order of the universe will bring peace to us." It is *shalom,* the peace of the living and not that of the grave. A prayer that begins with the magnificent sanctification of God's glory, a reaffirmation of man's faith.

God is not absent in death. Far from it, He is everlastingly present. He is the God of justice, the God of Job: "The Lord gave and the Lord has taken away; blessed be the name of the Lord." And He is the Lord of mercy, the Lord of David and the Psalms: "Yea, though I walk through the valley of the shadow of death, I will fear no evil, for Thou art with me; Thy rod and Thy staff, they comfort me."

God's presence is felt in the courage it bestows upon those who are asked to confront life without their loved one and in the comfort it gives to the bereaved. Hallow and extol, laud and exalt, honor and revere, adore and worship God—this is the message of the *Kaddish.* How often have I sensed a feeling of calmness, even of serenity and peace, descend upon the bereaved at the grave site after they recite.

It occurred to me during the drive home that emotionally I had been an intense mourner for two years, and in a certain sense I had also been the deceased. Michael was not dead, far from it, but my ambitions for him, my childish dreams and imaginings, my heroics certainly were. In my black despair, I had thought of Michael as worse than dead, living out his life as an adult with the mentality of a two-year-old, unable to speak or clothe himself, eternally dependent upon others.

During these two years I had lost faith in humanity because some of the people I encountered were coldly indifferent to Michael and his fate. I had lost faith in myself because I could see only the blackest of possibilities and because I was impatient and immature, dreaming of heroics without understanding the meaning of heroism.

Virginia Matson had not changed the insensibility of others, but she had shown me that some are equally capable of loving humanity. Nothing she said directly restored my faith in myself, but the future no longer looked so black and I did not feel overwhelmed by my tragedy.

Perhaps all the eight months of wandering and searching from school to school was leading up to the moment when I would drive to Deerfield, walk into the Grove School, and meet Virginia Matson.

At noontime of that same day, I walked into the small chapel of my congregation in Aurora, opened the ark, and said, "Thank You, God."

I realized then that God had not absented Himself from me during the two black years of my emotional turmoil and loss of faith. He had answered me, but I had not understood. I had asked for a miracle without comprehending the circumstance of the miracle. I had asked for the miracle of a medicine granting Michael intelligence, self-control, and emotional maturity. I, therefore, could not perceive the miracle that could be wrought by love.

180

20
God's Presence

I could feel God's presence. I could see love change Michael from a sullen child to a joyous one. Finally, I could begin to comprehend the self-destructive nature of my emotions and try to alter them.

In place of self-pity came compassion.

I have never been able stoically to accept all of life's trials with complete faith and say, "This, too, is for the good." I still can't stop the occasional daydream that begins, *If only Mike were a normal child, or if only a scientist could discover a cure for brain damage and hyperactivity*.... Yet I have learned that only through living with pain, sorrow, sadness, and personal tragedy can one learn to be compassionate.

I remember how impressed I was as a young child by a beautiful story my teacher told us about Moses, a story based upon an ancient rabbinic tradition. "God, the rabbis tell us," the teacher said, "never gives an important job to a person unless He first tests him in small matters. When feeding Jethro's sheep, Moses saw that a little lamb had wandered away from the flock. He followed it and overtook it at a brook quenching its thirst. 'Had I known,' Moses said to the lamb, 'I would have taken you in my arms and carried you to the brook.' God then said, 'Moses, you are fit to shepherd My people Israel.' "

Our teacher continued to explain that this small act of compassion toward a lamb had shown Moses' beautiful nature. For a few weeks afterward, whenever my friends or I found a stray kitten, we fed and tried to care for it. But it never prevented us from being cruel to each other as children usually are.

When as a young rabbi in Detroit I visited a terminally sick patient or bereaved parent, I found I could utter only the most commonplace and at times inane words of consolation. Intellectually I understood their grief and I sympathized with them, but this did not seem sufficient. I remember paying a condolence call upon a rabbi whose young son had within a matter of days died tragically of leukemia. I wanted to comfort the parents, but all I could do was sit and look into space or at my hands.

Now I find an echo in my own heart of such grief. I understand those anguished words, "Why me?" and I can respond to them.

Jewish tradition seems to have recognized the fact that *compassion can only come from maturity and experience.* This was incorporated in the qualifications for cantor.

A cantor leads the congregation in chanting the Hebrew prayers, lending beauty to the service by virtue of his singing ability and serving as the messenger of the community in praying to God. As representative of those who cannot pray and as a spokesman for the congregants in their role as a united, integral community, the cantor prays in the language of the Bible and it is hoped, reaches God's ears. Traditionally he was, therefore, selected with great care. It was important for him to be a pious, God-fearing individual as well as one possessing a fine voice.

On the High Holy Days, however, one more qualification was added. The cantor could not be a bachelor, for it was assumed that only a married man, having the cares and worries of family life, could be compassionate enough to properly serve as the communal messenger to God. It is perhaps indicative of modern values that most synagogues today are not concerned with the cantor's marital status or piety as long as he has a beautiful voice.

In Exodus 33:18, Moses asks God: "Show me, I pray Thee, Thy glory." Later on (34:5-6) the answer comes. "And the Lord descended in the cloud, and stood with him there, and proclaimed the name of the Lord. And the Lord passed by before him, and proclaimed: 'The Lord, the Lord God, merciful and gracious, long-suffering, and abundant in goodness and truth.' " Judaism teaches man to imitate these godly attributes (*Imitatio Dei*). Just as God is compassionate, so must we, created in His image, be compassionate.

The beauty of Michael's smile, his first words, the miracle of his reading taught me to appreciate the joy and pleasure of life and the ongoing marvel of God's creations.

How remarkable it is to watch a baby at seven, eight, or nine months pull himself up, stand erect, hold onto the sides of his crib, and take a few tentative steps; fall down, pull himself up again, and try once more to walk. Yet unless the baby happens to be our first child or grandchild, most of us take these first steps for granted. Only when the child has cerebral palsy or some form of brain damage or is retarded, and he is three years old and has never taken one step, does walking become such a marvelous event.

Or let us consider the art of talking. Scientists have only now begun to investigate the intricacies of human speech. We know that babies first learn to speak by imitating the sounds they hear from those near and dear to them. That is why a deaf child must be taught to speak in an entirely different manner. But imitation is only the first and perhaps the easiest step in the process. How does the young child learn to put two words together in a coherent fashion, and then three, and then a sentence? The sentences are at first awkward, ungrammatical, but they make sense to parents attuned to their children's speech patterns. We know what they are trying to say. Science still is at a loss to supply the answers to these questions, yet we take our children's speech for granted, and at times we may even find it annoying.

Alexandra loves to talk. She becomes particularly gabby at dinner time. She talks to Steve or Mike, Frances or myself, or to no one in particular on any and all subjects. She is probably trying either to be the center attraction or to avoid eating her food. I become annoyed and say, "Alexandra, can't you please be quiet and close your mouth for just a few minutes?" And then I stop myself. What am I saying! Michael started speaking when he was five years old. Until that time, no doctor could assure me he would ever speak. How often in those years did I dream of hearing his voice? How often did I wonder what it would sound like? How often did I wake from these dreams thinking, *Perhaps I'll never hear his voice!*

Silence may be golden, but to the parent of a retarded child who doesn't speak or an autistic child who will not speak, it is a cruel adage.

As a young boy I attended a Jewish parochial school in Brooklyn. Every morning school started with the same prayer which I recited in Hebrew: "I thank You, ever living God, for reawakening my soul; great is Your mercy and Your faithfulness."

My teachers told me that when I went to sleep my soul flew up to heaven; there it was nightly examined and judged. When I awoke, it meant that God had, in His infinite mercy, returned my soul to me, and I must therefore start the day by thanking Him. As I grew older and learned that sleep was necessary for replenishing the body's strength and had nothing to do with death, the simple *Modeh Ani* prayer ("I thank You") lost its meaning. I was blind to the truly beautiful, simple, yet sublime nature of the prayer.

There were other similar prayers that I recited in Hebrew every morning by rote. At first I had only the foggiest notion of their meanings, and though in time I learned Hebrew language and grammar and the translation of these prayers, I still recited them automatically.

The crises of my life, the knowledge of Michael's handicap, altered all my preconceived ideas and shook the very foundation of my faith. Yet in spite of all my doubts, I continued to put on my *tefillin* and say my prayers.

Now these prayers take on a new meaning.

"Blessed art Thou, O Lord our God, King of the universe, who openest the eyes of the blind."

Thank You, O Lord, for my eyes and my sight. Thank You for my ability to see and appreciate every morning, the beauty and wonder of nature, the earth, grass, flowers, snow, rain, to see those that I love, to read Your prayer books and study Your Bible. I hope I shall be able to go through life, eyes open and not blind to my duties, obligations, and responsibilities as a human being and a servant of God.

"Blessed art Thou, O Lord our God, King of the universe, who has made me in Thine image."

Thank You, O Lord, for my soul, the spark within me made in Thy divine image. Thank You for my conscience, the mechanism within me that can enable me to choose between right and wrong and thereby rise above the mundane in life to perform the most sacred of Thy tasks.

"Blessed art Thou, O Lord our God, King of the universe, who raisest up them that are bowed down."

Thank You, O Lord, for raising me from the depths of despair and dejection. For two years I had lost sight of You, denying Your existence, isolating myself from Your comforting presence. How foolish and miserable I was! Thank You for remaining ever near, and finally when my eyes were opened and I was not blinded by self-pity, You stretched out Your hand to me and I was no longer alone, no longer without consolation, no longer ashamed, no longer friendless or bowed down.

Weeks may go by and I will revert to my old habit of automatically reciting the prayers without consciously expressing these thoughts. Then one morning I open my eyes, see the words of the prayers, and comprehend the sublime beauty of their expression. I see my children in a different light: Michael going to school, reading, writing, working on simple arithmetic, and—wonder of wonders—speaking. Steve is tinkering with his Erector set, ice skating, enjoying school, and doing well in it, and Alexandra is skipping off to first grade, singing, dancing, her long brown tresses flowing in the breeze as she runs to play with her friends. I thank God for these lovely children, for my beautiful, courageous wife, and for the ability God has given me to enjoy the wonders of life.

Finally, I have had to rethink my own role as a father. Judaism has traditionally emphasized strong family ties, with the role of parents and children clearly defined. The children are to obey their parents; the commandment to "honor thy father and thy mother" is but one of many biblical injunctions. Parents are to educate their children ("Thou shalt teach them diligently unto thy children") and discipline them with tender affection. As the great eighteenth-century Rabbi Eliyah Gaon wrote, "When you lead your sons and daughters in the good way, let your words be tender and caressing in terms of disciplines that win the heart's assent."

In the process of educating and disciplining me, my parents had bequeathed to me a considerable psychological and moral legacy: a deep loyalty to Judaism, a strong conscience with an overdeveloped sense of guilt, a great love of reading and learning, and a desire to succeed.

I had accepted these values and hoped to project them to my children without consciously asking myself, "Have I been happy or satisfied with these values? Are there others that would be more important?"

There is a Hasidic tale about a saintly Rabbi Zusya who was dying and had gathered his students around him for the last time. They did not want to speak of his approaching death, but he knew his time had come and that he would shortly be meeting his Maker. "I am afraid of but one thing," Rabbi Zusya said as he prepared himself and his disciples for the end. "I am afraid of that moment when my soul will stand before the Lord on the Judgment Day. The prosecuting angel, who will be presenting my case before the eternal Judge, will not ask me why I was not an Abraham or a Moses. But the prosecuting angel will ask me why was I not a Zusya? Why had I not lived up to my own capabilities?"

I hope I will be able to instill in my children a loyalty to Judaism, a knowledge of right and wrong, the desire to do right out of love, not fear, and a respect for learning. What of success? I pray that they develop their inherent potentialities. The success I treasured was built upon the ephemeral and corrupt values of a materialistic society. It brought me no happiness. It was a false dream and it is best that I broke with it.

Milestones

21
The Bar Mitzvah

The Bar Mitzvah is a milestone in the life of a Jewish boy. At the age of thirteen and a day, he takes upon himself the prerogatives and responsibilities of an adult. He literally becomes a *bar mitzvah* ("master of the commandment"). He is counted towards a *minyan,* the quorum of ten men necessary to conduct a service, and he may be called to recite the blessings over the Torah scroll. According to an ancient Jewish tradition, parents are responsible for their son's actions only until he reaches the age of thirteen.

Since girls mature more quickly, they come of age according to Jewish tradition at twelve. However, in most synagogues, her Bat Mitzvah is at thirteen.

Psychologically, the Bar Mitzvah service is one of the most important moments in the boy's adolescence. During the day, he is the center of attraction. While he conducts the service at temple all eyes are focused upon him.

Preparations are intensive. He must know Hebrew. He must know how to chant a lengthy portion of the Bible. On the Saturday morning of his Bar Mitzvah, he, his family, friends, and relatives will gather at the temple for services, where he will be called to the Torah to chant his part. The more knowledgeable and willing boys may conduct part or all of the services in Hebrew.

The youngster has worked hard to prepare for this moment. As he stands at the ark chanting the ancient Hebrew in the Bible, he feels rightfully proud of his accomplishments. Judaism acknowledges him as a man. He knows that he is no longer a child.

I can recall quite vividly my own Bar Mitzvah. I spent months studying in preparation for the service. A month before, my parents took me to a department store, where we purchased my first suit. For days before the Sabbath my mother and a friend cooked and baked the food and cakes that would be served to all the congregants and guests following the services. I shall never understand how seventy adults and ten children could have been squeezed into and served in our living room that had previously accommodated fifteen at the maximum. I can still see the pride shining in my parents' eyes after I had completed the services, the sense of accomplishment and joy in my heart.

What of a Bar Mitzvah for Michael? Had the suggestion been made before he began attending the Grove School, I would have thought it ludicrous. This child who could not speak, who was so hyperactive that most special-education schools had refused to accept him—a candidate for Bar Mitzvah? Impossible!

Time passed. He started speaking and, miracle of miracles, learned to read. His love of music and his ability to learn and remember tunes enabled him to memorize the Friday evening *Kiddush,* the Chanukah blessings, the Four Questions of Passover, and a few simple prayers in Hebrew. When he was eleven my congregation presented us with a trip to Israel. During that stay Michael learned a few simple Hebrew words such as *abah* and *imah* ("father" and "mother").

But I had never contemplated giving him a formal Hebrew education, for I knew how impossible it would be for him to attend Hebrew school with normal children, even those far younger than himself.

One day when Michael turned twelve I said to Frances,

"Why shouldn't I try to teach Mike to read Hebrew? Reading English has never been a problem with him. Perhaps he can learn a second language as well."

"Fine," she replied, "if you want to try, but you know how frustrating it can become getting him to do some work."

The next evening after supper I sat down to work with him. He had watched me teach Steve to read Hebrew when he was seven; I told Michael that it was now his turn. If he knew Hebrew he would enjoy Friday night and Saturday morning services. He agreed to try.

It is not as difficult to learn Hebrew as it seems. The alphabet dates back some three thousand years to the ancient Near East and the Israel of David and Solomon, the Maccabees and Hillel. The characters are read from right to left and the vowels are the dots and dashes found beneath the consonants. Unlike English, Hebrew is a perfectly phonetic language. To master it requires a decent memory and the ability to concentrate.

Michael had a fine memory—but what of his concentration? Could such a hyperactive child control himself and focus his attention on the work at hand? Furthermore, would learning another language confuse him and harm him in his English studies? In my years of teaching Hebrew both to children and adults, I had never had a student drop out of my class because of confusion with such an alien language, but Michael was not the average normal child. I was most worried, however, about the actual method of instruction. I had tried to help him with his homework, but usually with disastrous results. He balked at my aid and insisted he couldn't do the work. In turn I would become frustrated and lose my temper. In the past I had never had any success working with him. Would I now?

The first evening's work went along smoothly. He quickly learned two letters of the alphabet and their sounds. He was interested in doing the work and quite pleased with himself.

The second evening was much more trying. He didn't want to repeat last night's work. He wanted to move ahead. I persisted and he grew angry. I cajoled, threatened, and he threw a tantrum. Finally after a half-hour he had completed but one line of new work. The third and fourth nights were repetitions of the second.

I had been afraid of this. The old pattern was back. Yet deep within me I felt he could learn Hebrew if only he realized that we expected this of him and he expended some effort.

Friday night after the Sabbath meal I called him into the living room for a man-to-man talk. "Mike," I said, "I know you can learn Hebrew if you want to—you must do it. I am not going to give up trying, and I want and expect you to help." We walked back into the kitchen, I opened the Hebrew primer, and we began our nightly lesson. This time it was easier. He covered two lines instead of one and it took him fifteen minutes, not thirty. He did it with less resistance and fewer mistakes.

We went along in this manner for weeks. Some evenings he was cooperative, while at other times I almost gave up. However, we persisted and in a few months had finished the primer. As a reward we gave him his own prayer book.

When I told Virginia Matson about his feat, she said, "That's almost miraculous. Children with Michael's auditory problems never learn a second language. It's too confusing. He's quite unusual, isn't he?"

Learning rudiments of Hebrew added to his sense of accomplishments and self-confidence, but it was only a small step toward preparing for a Bar Mitzvah. The Bar Mitzvah boy prepares and chants fluently a chapter or more from the Bible in Hebrew as well as a number of blessings also in Hebrew. He has usually had four or five years of weekly Hebrew studies. For Michael to move from the primer to the Bar Mitzvah lessons would be comparable to a foreign student learning the simple English of the Dick-and-Jane readers and following this with a chapter of the Bible in the King James Version.

I also had to take into consideration Michael's unique problems. The Bar Mitzvah is a time of nervous strain for the most normal of children. How would a hyperactive child react to the tension? Every time Mike had participated in a class play, he had stood on stage visibly frightened and had never performed properly. The Bar Mitzvah would mean standing by himself at the ark and chanting prayers in a foreign language before hundreds of people.

I hadn't mentioned the possibility of a Bar Mitzvah to Frances when I first began to work with Michael. I tried not to think of it. I told Frances that since Mike had seemed interested in Hebrew when I taught Steve, and since he could read English, I should try to teach him Hebrew.

Now, however, I mentioned the prospect.

"Hy, I just don't know," she replied. "Why don't you talk it over with Virginia? She's had other Jewish children. Perhaps she can suggest something."

Mrs. Matson's answer was not what I had expected. It was neither a yes nor a no. "Rabbi, doesn't the Bar Mitzvah also depend on a certain maturity? Shouldn't the boy be emotionally mature enough so that this service marks the end of his childhood and the beginning of his adolescence?" She was right. Though the rabbis had made Bar Mitzvah conditional on age, they were concerned as well with maturity. In ancient times the thirteen-year-old was expected to do the chores of an adult and behave as an adult. An orphan had his Bar Mitzvah a year sooner because the family responsibility devolved upon him at an earlier age. Very few if any Jewish young boys go to work today at the age of thirteen, but this is certainly a year in which they mature physically, psychologically, and emotionally and are no longer children. This wasn't true of Michael. Emotionally he was at least four years younger. Why not postpone a Bar Mitzvah until he had matured somewhat? Perhaps, as Virginia had suggested, "Wait for another few years."

Frances and I both agreed that this was wise.

Yet the spark of an idea still remained. Mike was going to be thirteen in four months. He was our oldest son, our first-born. Perhaps we should try a modified Bar Mitzvah, some sort of brief ceremony that would indicate to him that his status had changed, that Judaism considered him a man in spite of his afflictions and handicaps.

There was just such a service. What we in the United States viewed as an abbreviated service was in fact the service for the majority of thirteen-year-olds in Europe up to the twentieth century. When the boy had reached Bar Mitzvah age, he would be taken by his father to the synagogue usually on a Monday or Thursday morning, be called up to the Torah, chant two short blessings, and then sit down.

Perhaps we could follow the same procedure with Michael. On the Saturday after his thirteenth birthday we would take him to temple with us, call him to the Torah, and have him recite the blessings. We would make it as simple as possible, notify no one of our intentions, and put as little strain on our son as possible. Frances agreed it was worth a trial.

I promptly sat down with Michael and told him his mother and I wanted him to have a Bar Mitzvah. He had attended others and he knew that when a Jewish boy was thirteen, he had this service. He would soon be thirteen, and he would also have a Bar Mitzvah. However, his would not be elaborate. We would have it in the chapel rather than the sanctuary and few people would be there so that he needn't be frightened or worried. But we expected him to prepare for the day and to do as fine a job as he could.

The actual preparation for Michael proved simple. We purchased a record of a cantor singing the blessings. Every evening for three weeks Mike listened to the record while he followed the words in the prayer book. I then had him chant it for me without benefit of the record. In a short time, he had memorized the six lines of the Hebrew blessings.

Finally the Saturday of Michael's Bar Mitzvah arrived. We made no announcement of the event. A few of our dearest friends found out and asked us if we minded their coming. "Of course not," we said and then explained that we didn't want to make a big thing of it and so we were keeping it low-key.

Frances' mother, brother, sister-in-law, and their children spent the Sabbath with us so they too could attend.

The day was beautiful, a fine pleasant autumn Sabbath. We walked together to the temple, all the while impressing on Michael that he was no longer a child and should do the best that he could. I sat on the *bimah* ("pulpit") while Mike sat next to his mother, brother, and sister. The congregation chanted the psalms, read the prayers, and the cantor took the Torah scroll from the ark. He placed it on the table, and I began to read the week's portion of the Bible from it. First we called the *kohen* ("priest"), who walked to the table with his prayer shawl, kissed the Torah, and then chanted the blessings. Then we called the Levite and four other adults.

Michael's turn had finally arrived. I called him up to the *bimah* by his Hebrew name, which is Menashe Ben Zion, the name of my late grandfather. I had told myself that there was nothing to be nervous about. It really didn't matter if Michael chanted the blessings or not. Yet when I called his name I could feel my heart palpitating. And I became more tense when he stood, took a few steps toward the Torah, and then turned and began walking back to his mother. As he reached Frances he bent down to say in a voice that could be heard by those sitting next to her: *"Trust me, Mom!"* He turned around, walked to the Torah, took the fringes of his prayer shawl in hand, kissed the Torah, and began to chant the prayers in a soft and beautiful voice.

When he concluded, there were tears in the eyes of all present, particularly in mine and his mother's. He stood at the table tall, straight, and proud. After services we told him how proud we were of him. In the eyes of the people and in our eyes, he was no longer a child. As I walked home with Frances, I said, "He proved he can do it. I think we should begin planning for another Bar Mitzvah—we would invite all his friends, teachers, relatives, and the congregation. He deserves the same Bar Mitzvah as a normal boy. Look how proud he seems. We must show him that we truly trust him."

22
"Heal Me, O Lord"

We now set to work preparing for Michael's Bar Mitzvah with renewed vigor and anticipation. We settled on Saturday, May 26, 1973. This would give Michael six months to prepare the blessings and the *Haftarah*, the portion of the prophets that he was to chant. May 26 was also part of the Memorial Day weekend, and we were hoping that Ruth Shusterman, a very dear friend of ours who lived in Detroit and had known Michael since birth, would come.

Frances drew up the list for the invitations and began planning the menu with the caterer. (Gone were the days when the mother, together with a few friends, prepared the food for the party.) We anticipated over two hundred adults at the services, and we wanted to invite all our guests to a luncheon in the temple social hall following.

I obtained the special booklet that contained the *Haftarah* as well as the blessings. As I had done with the brief blessings back in October, I taped the complete service on a cassette.

Michael, of course, had the most difficult chore. As I anticipated, he enjoyed playing the cassette and chanting along with the tape. He did not like the practice sessions, though he quickly learned the melody and had no great difficulty with the words.

Weeks flew by. A relatively mild winter was followed by a rainy, chilly, cold spring. As the day drew near I took Michael to the temple and had him practice in the sanctuary, standing at the reading table near the ark as he would do for the service. He did fairly well at these practice sessions, and we kept telling him how beautifully he was doing in order to build up his confidence. However, we could not duplicate the actual conditions, the hundreds of people in the sanctuary, and the tension any child or adult would feel at that moment.

The Sunday before his Bar Mitzvah, I brought the tape recorder to the temple to record Michael chanting the service for my mother living in Israel. Michael froze at the sight of the recorder and the knowledge that the tape would be sent to Israel. He stood staring at the microphone, and when he finally began chanting the blessing, it was in a low, almost inaudible voice. We had to re-record it a number of times before we obtained a serviceable tape. Would this happen on Saturday? Would he freeze when he looked out at the audience and saw the sea of faces before him?

We awoke early Saturday morning to a bright and sunny day. The weatherman had threatened rain, but nature seemed to be smiling upon Michael. Fortunately for Frances, we had a house full of company, my in-laws, their children, and Ruth from Detroit. She was so busy with the company that she had little time to worry about Mike.

He seemed calm, aware of the day's importance, and prepared to do his best. He sat with Frances while I sat on the *bimah*. Frances' brother was the cantor leading the congregation in singing the Hebrew portions of the service. Every so often I looked down at Michael, who seemed unperturbed and absorbed in the service. He stood when the congregation did and quietly sang those parts he knew. I had been taking him to Saturday morning services for the past two years and he had grown quite familiar with it. But he always teased me at these services, refusing to stand when the congregation did, skipping pages, whispering to me, turning around and smiling at his neighbors. This morning he was all concentration, closely following the service and only occasionally talking to his mother.

The Torah scroll was taken from the ark, placed on the reading table, and I started chanting the scriptural portion of the week. First the *kohen* and then the Levite were called to chant the Torah blessings. Traditionally relatives of the Bar Mitzvah boy are called to the Torah on this occasion, and so Michael's uncles, some of our dear friends, and I said our blessings.

Finally the moment came for Michael to be called. I had kept telling myself, *It really doesn't matter how well he performs. Everyone in the congregation knows him; however well he does will be a great accomplishment.* But I didn't believe all that. I so wanted Michael to do well, for his sake more than for my own.

He began his chanting, and it was as if the congregation held its collective breath. As he sang the final words, there was an audible sigh of relief and joy in the audience. Michael had chanted his service beautifully. He had sung it loudly, clearly, and correctly. He had done himself proud.

It had been a long and hard road to this day. At one time I had despaired of ever hearing Michael talk or sit still during a service. This Saturday he had chanted a portion of the prophets in Hebrew and had helped conduct the services, also in Hebrew.

Every Saturday I deliver a sermon. Customarily on a Sabbath when there is a Bar Mitzvah I address myself to the boy and his parents. This Saturday, I felt I could not deliver a sermon but that I must express something of what I felt to the audience. I began by saying, "I now know how parents of other Bar Mitzvah boys feel." I intended to acknowledge people in the audience who had done so much for Michael— his past and present teachers, the director of pupil personnel, and in particular Virginia Matson. But I could not. My throat grew dry, tears welled up in my eyes, and I began to sob. I was so proud of Michael. This day had been such a joyful and spiritual occasion that I could not control my emotions.

There was yet one other whose help I needed to acknowledge. Significantly this acknowledgment was contained in the prophetic portion Michael had chanted: Jeremiah 16:19-17:14, which is chanted each year on this particular Sabbath. We had chosen this day for entirely different reasons, yet as I read from Jeremiah I realized how relevant it was for our purpose. It was as if the prophet were speaking to me.

It begins with "O Lord, my strength, and my stronghold, and my refuge in the day of affliction." And it concludes with the heartrending prayer later included by the rabbis in the daily liturgy: "Heal me, O Lord, and I shall be healed; save me, and I shall be saved, for Thou art my praise."